Art and Value

For my grandmother, Martha Augusta Brown

Art and Value

George Dickie

BLACKWELL
Publishers

First published 2001

2 4 6 8 10 9 7 5 3 1

Blackwell Publishers Inc.
350 Main Street
Malden, Massachusetts 02148
USA

Blackwell Publishers Ltd
108 Cowley Road
Oxford OX4 1JF
UK

Library of Congress Cataloging-in-Publication Data
Dickie, George, 1926–
Art and value: themes in the philosophy of art/George Dickie.
p. cm.
Includes bibliographical references and index.
ISBN 0-631-22945-0 (hb: alk. paper)—ISBN 0-631-22946-9 (pb.: alk. paper)
1. Art—Philosophy. 2. Values. I. Title. .
N66 .D5 2001
700'.1—dc21
2001025693

British Library Cataloguing in Publication Data
A CIP catalogue record for this book is available from the British Library.

Typeset in 10½ on 13 pt Bembo
by Best-set Typesetter Ltd., Hong Kong
Printed in Great Britain by MPG Books, Bodmin, Cornwall

This book is printed on acid-free paper.

Contents

Acknowledgments

Chapter 2, "Methodological Background of the Philosophy of Art," in a slightly different form, will also appear as an essay in the forthcoming *Blackwell Guide to Aesthetics*, edited by Peter Kivy. Chapter 3, "Nature of Art Theories," in a somewhat different form first appeared as an essay in *The Journal of Aesthetics and Art Criticism*, Winter 1997, and is reprinted with the permission of Blackwell Publishers. The first two-thirds of chapter 4, "History of the Institutional Theory," in a somewhat different form first appeared as an essay in *Theories of Art Today*, © 2000, edited by Noël Carroll and is reprinted by permission of The University of Wisconsin Press. The last third of chapter 4 in a somewhat different form first appeared in the *British Journal of Aesthetics*, April 1998, and is reprinted with the permission of Oxford University Press. The last two-thirds of chapter 5 first appeared as an essay in the *British Journal of Aesthetics*, July 1999, and is reprinted with the permission of Oxford University Press. Chapter 6 in a slightly different form first appeared in the *British Journal of Aesthetics*, April 2000, and is reprinted with the permission of Oxford University Press.

Special thanks are due to Jeffrey Dean, acquitions editor for Blackwell Publishers, and Anthony Grahame who copy-edited this book.

Introduction

The topics of the chapters of this book in one way or another revolve around the institutional theory of art. In chapter 1, the topic is the role that teleology has played as an explicit or an implicit presupposition in theorizing about the nature of art. Many anti-teleological philosophers have proceeded in the "teleological manner" despite their explicitly naturalistic overall view of the nature of the world. The view that these naturalistic philosophies and the teleological philosophers had in common is the presupposition that the nature of art can be discovered embedded in the mechanisms of human nature. In the cases of many of the earlier philosophers, the mechanisms are viewed as divinely implanted. Even when the teleological philosophers do not have such theological views, they have continued to seek for *psychological* theories by focusing on the mechanisms of human nature. The *cultural* theories of art of Arthur Danto's "The Artworld," the institutional theory, and theories of this type, find no place for the 'teleological manner.'

Chapter 2 begins with a discussion of Plato's metaphysics and philosophy of langauge as a background for theorizing about the meaning of words and specifically about the meaning of 'art.' I then discuss the metaphysics of Plato's ancient rivals, the Greek atomists, whose views contrast so sharply with his. I note that the atomists did not have a philosophy of language to compete with Plato's and that, consequently, Plato influenced the method of defining meanings and the atomists did not. Shifting to the present, I discuss James Carney's attempt to apply the Kripke/Putnam view of proper names and natural kinds to the problem of the definition of "art," noting that the Kripke/Putnam view of reality is a modern update of the Greek atomists' view of reality. But unlike their ancient counterparts, the Kripke/Putnam ties an explicit philosophy of language to their scientific view of reality. I discuss and accept Peter Kivy's and Thomas Leddy's criticisms of Carney's view. I then go on to try to apply to the problem of the definition of art a scaled-down version of the Kripke/Putnam extensional view that does not involve necessity and views art as a cultural, institutional thing.

Chapter 3 begins by taking note of Stephen Davies's classification of theories of art into procedural, functional, and historical. In the first part of this chapter I discuss most of the same theories that he does in his book *Definitions of Art* in terms of his categories and in the light of his analyses and criticisms. I am especially concerned with Davies's own institutional version of the nature of art and with his criticism of my institutional theory. I argue that his version of the institutional theory, which makes the notion of authority central, is wrong. In the second part of this chapter, although I find no fault with Davies's scheme for classifying theories of art, I introduce an alternative way of classifying them according to whether they are natural-kind theories or cultural-kind theories, such as the institutional account of art. This second way of classifying is related to the psychological/cultural distinction used in chapter 1.

Chapter 4 runs over the history of my earlier and later versions of the institutional theory of art. The earlier version was refined through a series of articles and book sections in response to various criticisms. The later version was also a response to criticism but it marked a substantial change in the nature of the theory. In the last part of this chapter, I respond to a criticism of the institutional theory by Wollheim that is widely believed to be fatal to the theory. I argue that Wollheim's argument does not work at all.

Chapter 5 focuses directly on the question of how art is evaluated. I summarize the main topics of my 1988 book, *Evaluating Art*, and then respond to three extensive criticisms of the book.

In chapter 6, I discuss the question of whether the concept of art is an evaluative notion as so many philosophers have maintained or whether it is a neutral notion as the institutional theory has claimed. I conclude that the concept is not an evaluative one but that works of art, unlike some things, fall into the category of evaluable things.

1

Historical Background of the Philosophy of Art

Once we break with an old way of doing something and find a new way of doing it, we may be able to see the old way in a whole new light. Things about the old way may then be revealed that we could not have noticed before or could have noticed only with exceptional insight. Such is the case now in aesthetics with regard to the sphere of theories that deal with the nature of art. We can now see that philosophers theorized about the nature of art with a certain underlying assumption from ancient Greek times to approximately the middle of the twentieth-century. This centuries-old assumption – an assumption I hope to undermine – is that the basic nature of art derives directly from distinctive innate mechanisms embedded in human nature. I shall call these innate features 'psychological mechanisms.' By the way, I am not suggesting that there are no innate psychological mechanisms that function in connection with art; obviously, there are – sensory and motor mechanisms, for example. I am concerned only with those psychological mechanisms alleged to be specifically and sufficiently productive of art. Throughout the great bulk of the history of philosophy, philosophers have relied on psychological mechanisms to construct what I shall call 'psychological theories of art.' Once we notice this, the history of the philosophy of art become a whole new history.

The first theory of art – the imitation theory – is a psychological theory. The imitation theory – despite being invented or adopted by Plato in an attempt to discredit art – caught on and held on as conventional wisdom for some two thousand years, largely because of the inattention of philosophers. Aristotle, who unlike Plato takes a positive view of art, makes clear that the mechanism that the imitation theory uses to charac-

terize art is conceived of as innate by his claiming that imitating is something that people *naturally* do and *naturally* delight in.

For Aristotle, the innate mechanism for imitating and any other innate
mechanisms were parts of a larger teleological order of things, so that
for him the creation of art was simply one more item in nature's purpo-
sive scheme. Beginning with the Christian era and on up until relatively
recently, the prevailing philosophical approach was to preserve the notion
of the world as a teleological order and to nest it within a larger theological context. So, during the bulk of two-thousand-year reign of the
imitation theory of art, the psychological mechanism that was held to be
responsible for the creation of art was conceived of by almost all thinkers
as the carefully crafted creation of a benevolent deity. This kind of
teleological–theological theorizing is shown very clearly, for example,
in the theory of taste of the eighteenth-century philosopher Francis
Hutcheson. Hutcheson claims that the innate mechanism that for him
makes up the faculty of taste was created by a benevolent deity to provide
human beings with pleasure in their lives. Hutcheson also held the imitation theory of art, which because he viewed it as conventional wisdom,
he neither explained or defended. If he had explained it, he would have
claimed that a benevolent deity had implanted the imitating mechanism
for the creation of art for our pleasure and edification.

Finally, in the nineteenth century, philosophers apparently noticed that
some imitations are not art and that some artwork are not imitations; the
imitation theory was then at long last replaced when Romanticism gave
birth to the expression theory of art – the view that the expression of
emotion is either a necessary condition of art or is identical with art. The
expression theory of art then became unquestioned conventional wisdom
until well into the twentieth century. For example, in 1934, John Dewey,
without any supporting argument, set forth a version of the expression
theory. In 1938, R. G. Collingwood felt he could argue that since English-
speakers hold art to be spontaneous, *and* the controlled expression of
emotion *is* spontaneous, that he could reasonably conclude that art *is identical* with the controlled expression of emotion.

Whatever one thinks of Dewey's nonargument or Collingwood's invalid
argument, what I want to focus on is the fact that expressionists partially
or wholly define "art" using only the psychological mechanism of the controlled expression of emotion. These theorists place art in the same domain
with the specifically aimed growl of a dog with a bone. And, they make
the creation of art analogous to the production of bowers by male bower
birds, something these birds do as a result of their innate natures and appar-

ently without a plan in mind. Note that the production of bowers is an integral part of the reproductive behavior of bower birds, which from an evolutionary point of view ties the production of bowers closely to the instinctual nature of the birds. By the way, I am not suggesting that the urges to imitate and to express emotion are in any way bogus or that expressing emotion or imitating cannot be involved in the creation of art. I and many others have, however, argued that neither imitation nor the expression of emotion is sufficient or necessary for defining art.

The last psychological theory of art I shall mention at this initial stage is Monroe Beardsley's, which was presented in 1979. Beardsley wrote that an artwork is "an intentional arrangement of conditions for affording experiences with marked aesthetic character."[1] Beardsley believed that pieces like *Fountain*, which Duchamp made using a urinal, are not works of art because Duchamp and his ilk had the wrong intentions. The central notions of Beardsley's definition are *intentional action* and *experience with marked aesthetic character*. Intentional action is a purely psychological notion. Beardsley characterizes experience with marked aesthetic character using only psychological notions, namely, Dewey's notion of coherent experience, Bullough's notion of detached experience, and the notion of the perception of the aesthetic qualities of unity, intensity, and complexity. Beardsley's theory of art presupposes that the creation of art can be explained by the citing of only innate psychological notions.

Dewey, Collingwood, Beardsley, and other philosophers of art of the twentieth century were assuming without realizing it that psychological mechanisms inherent in human nature all by themselves were sufficient for the production of art. These philosophers, or at least the great bulk of them, did not hold any teleological view of nature. Many of them explicitly rejected teleology. But in identifying art wholly or partially with the product of a psychological mechanism, these philosophers were theorizing as if they believed as earlier philosophers had that the production of artworks is teleologically determined by psychological mechanisms implanted by a benevolent deity. If these present-day philosophers of art had taken the implications of Darwinian evolution − a completely non-teleological theory − seriously they would have realized that they had no assurance that our "hard-wired" natures can suffice for the production of art. There is no reason to think that the process of natural selection would have provided an innate mechanism or mechanisms that alone would be responsible for the production of art. Of course, many of our "hard-wired" aspects are involved in the invention and production of art, but more than they alone were needed to invent art.

From the early 1960s, a number of philosophers in the analytic tradition have attempted to resolve the problems of the nature of art with theories that rely in some degree on concepts of cultural context rather than simply on psychological concepts. The work of these philosophers had several hallmarks. One, they attacked the psychological notions that had been used in defining of "art" as inadequate to the task. Two, they attempted to describe some aspects of the defining characteristics of "art" in terms of artworks' cultural contexts, although they may not have explicitly conceived of these ideas as cultural notions. Cultural theorists thus break sharply with the traditions of the psychological theories. It is this break in the way that the nature of art is theorized about that allows us to see that the earlier theories were all psychological in nature.

I turn now to these cultural theories of art. Suzanne Langer was perhaps the first to use cultural-sounding language in attempting to define 'art,' when in the 1950s she claimed that art is "the creation of forms *symbolic* of human feeling." Considered as a cultural notion, however, there is a problem about symbolism as she conceives it. In response to criticism by Ernest Nagel,[2] Langer acknowledged that what she is calling 'symbolism' lacks any aspect of *convention*.[3] Consequently, her view amounts to the view that art is the creation of forms that merely *resemble* human feeling. By not employing the notion of convention and thus actual symbolism, she rules out the only apparent cultural element in her theory. Langer's theory in involving only resemblance turns out to be a version of the imitation theory and, hence, is a psychological theory.

In 1964, Arthur Danto in his article, "The Artworld," followed in the footsteps of his old teacher, Suzanne Langer, and characterized art in cultural-sounding language.[4] As it turns out, Danto is actually talking about what, if it occurred, would be cultural phenomena, although he does not explicitly characterize it as such. Danto introduced his theory with an argument that compares a series of pairs of perceptually-indiscernible objects – Duchamps's artwork *Fountain* and a nonartwork urinal, Warhol's artwork *Brillo Box* and a nonartwork actual brillo box, and so on. Since the artwork and the nonartwork in each pair are supposed to exactly resemble one another visually, it is concluded that some nonvisual thing must make *Fountain* and *Brillo Box* art. Danto then concludes that the nonvisual thing is an art theory that prevailed at the time; he mentions two such theories that have prevailed at different times – the imitation theory of art and what he calls the "real" theory of art, a theory that asserts that real things, i.e., nonimitations, can be artworks. According to Danto, a prevailing art theory "takes up an object into the artworld" and makes it art. (This is not all Danto has to say about the nature of art in his article, but it is what I want to focus on here.) Danto's theory of art is a kind of meta-theory that contains within it reference to the holding of "lower-level" theories of art that prevail at particular times. Various of the things that Danto says commit him, I believe, to the view that the phenomena his meta-theory of art refer to, namely, objects becoming art, were at work from the instant that the first lower-level theory of art, namely, the imitation theory, was formulated by a philosopher. I am not wholly clear about the details of the meta-theory set forth in Danto's "The Artworld," but I believe his theory is a cultural one because, according to it, art is supposedly art because of its relation to the prevailing theory of art that is held at the time. Any theory that contains reference to the holding of a prevailing theory by a group of people at a particular time has got to be a cultural one.

Some nine years after his "Artworld" article appeared, Danto published two articles that expressed a more Langer-like view in which *aboutness* is alleged to be a necessary condition of art.[5] In 1981, he published a book in which he continued to maintain the necessity of aboutness for art.[6] In 2000, he is still defending the aboutness of art, and I will examine his argument later. In any event, Danto had said in connection with the about-ness aspect of art that art is "a language of sorts."[7] Danto's later, Langer-like theory appears to have psychological elements with its reference to art as "a language of sorts" involving aboutness. In saying this, I am assuming that the aboutness aspect of language is a "hard-wired" human phe-nomenon, although of course many aspects of sophisticated languages that rest on this fundamental aboutness phenomenon are cultural inventions. Danto's later theory also appears to have a cultural element with its ref-erence to art history as essential. So Danto's later theory appears to be mixture of psychological and cultural elements as *necessary* elements that are jointly sufficient.[8]

Beginning in 1969, following the lead of Danto's "The Artworld," I began trying to formulate a cultural theory of art, but instead of focusing on the holding of 'lower-level' theories of art that 'took up' objects into an artworld, I took a more 'anthropological' approach and focused on the cultural phenomena of artworld practices and behaviors.[9] This point of view has come to be called "The Institutional Theory of Art." My final formulation in 1984 of the institutional theory can be encapsulated in its definition of 'work of art' – "A work of art is an artifact of a kind created to be presented to an artworld public."[10]

In 1991, in his book, *Definitions of Art*, Stephen Davies declares that he himself opts for an institutional approach.[11] Davies, however, only hints at what his view is by claiming that my version of the institutional theory is wrong because it lacks an account of the necessary element of *authority* that he asserts is required for someone to produce art. He is right that my view has no place for authority, but Davies has not himself yet attempted to set out any argument for his claim that institutional authority is required in producing art or attempted even to illustrate how artists exercise authority in creating art. It seems to me that the institutional practice of producing art is quite different from institutional practices involving authority such as the handing down of judicial decisions, the writing and filling of prescriptions, the awarding of degrees, and the like. It does not seem to me that in producing art artists exercise authority; they just do something that they have learned how to do.

Jerrold Levinson has set forth a theory that at least appears to have institutional and, hence, cultural elements. A work of art is, he writes, "an object connected in a particular manner, in the intention of a maker . . . with *preceding* art . . . the agent in question intend[ing] the object for regard . . . in some way or ways that what are acknowledged as already artworks, are or were correctly regarded."[12] This theory involves a temporal dimension in theorizing about the nature of art. Levinson says that an historical account such as his with its temporal aspect requires a starting point, namely, what he calls Ur-art and which he at first stipulates to be art. Later, he has second thoughts about stipulation and says that either Ur-art is art because all subsequent art sprang from it or Ur-art is not art and the first art derived from Ur-art is different from all the art that comes after first art. Perhaps there is a problem here, but in any event his theory does appear to contain at least one cultural element in that it involves a notion of the *correct regard* of earlier artworks. Levinson tests the limits of correct regard by imagining a person in a society that completely lacks art arranging colored stones and creating the first art in his or her society. This person's construction is art, Levinson says, because the person regards the arranged colored stones in a way that members of another culture of which he is completely ignorant regard their art. Levinson's theory envisages art being created by having someone intending that something be regarded in a way that preceding art was correctly regarded without that someone realizing that there is any preceding art that is correctly regarded. How, from the point of view of the arranger, would the envisaged case of the colored-stone arranger who happened to arrange his stones at a time when another culture existed that had a notion of correct regard differ from that of an arranger of colored stones at an earlier time when no culture had a notion of correct regard? The intentional states of the two imagined arrangers are identical and neither contains any hint of awareness of the cultural notion of correct regard even if in the one case there is correct regard somewhere else. (I shall discuss this aspect of Levinson's argument again in chapter 3.) It appears that Levinson's theory, like Beardsley's, is at bottom a psychological theory that depends on an appreciation of aesthetic qualities.

In conclusion, because the mechanisms assumed by the psychological theories are conceived of as innate or treated as if they are, they are conceived of as determining behaviors and undergoings that result from features that individuals have independently of their *particular* cultural context, although of course every human behavior or undergoing takes place within some culture or other. Neither the pre-1960s philosophers nor Beardsley or Levinson would have denied that human beings are cultural beings or would have denied that art exists in some cultural context. When, however, these philosophers come to the point of saying what art fundamentally is, they refer only to psychological mechanisms such as the expression of emotion or the experience of aesthetic qualities. (Danto's later theory, as noted, is a mixture of psychological and cultural elements.) Thus, these philosophers assumed, perhaps in many cases without being self-consciously aware of it, that human beings come equipped with faculties, dispositions, and/or characteristics that suffice for the creation of art. Most earlier philosophers assumed that an omniscient, omnipotent God had had the foresight to create human beings with the hard-wired equipment that would suffice for the creation of art or, in the absence of an explicit theological background, that there was some kind of natural teleology of the kind that Aristotle assumed. That psychological mechanisms would suffice for the production of art is plausible if those mechanisms are supplied by a deity with a benevolent and encompasing plan in mind or if they occur within an explicit teleological context. But with neither of these contexts to rely on, the confidence that innate mechanisms might suffice is not assured. Theorizing that depended solely on psychological mechanisms persisted even after the theological and teleological background was no longer explicitly invoked.

There is, by the way, one psychological mechanism that either explicitly or implicitly will necessarily be involved in the creation of art which should be mentioned – and that is intentional action. Danto's early theory and the institutional theory presuppose the psychological mechanism of intentional action. The artists, the art-theory-holders, and artworld publics referred to by these two theories all engage in intentional action. The use of the psychological mechanism of intentional action seems unavoidable by any theory of art.

The central insight of the cultural approach is that art is a collective *invention* of human beings and not something that an artist produces simply out of his or her biological nature as a spider does a web or as a bower bird does a bower. The production of an artwork, unlike the production of a bower, does not appear to be directly connected to behavior closely tied to the evolutionary process as the bower of a bower bird clearly is because of its role in the reproductive process.

Before the 1960s, all philosophers presupposed that a certain repertory of ideas about psychological mechanisms were to be used in conceptualizing the creation of art. This was true of some philosophers even after the 1960s. The psychological theories of these philosophers have their origin in a teleological understanding of human beings and their environment. Arguments that refuted the psychological theories with their obsolete teleological assumptions paved the way for the use of a new repertory of cultural concepts for theorizing about the creation of art. Each of the cultural theories discussed may be inadequate in one way or another, but they mark a radical change in the way that many of us now theorize about art.

Notes

1 Monroe Beardsley, "In Defense of Aesthetic Value," *Proceedings and Addresses of the American Philosophical Association*, Newark, Del., American Philosophical Association, 1979, p. 729.
2 Earnest Nagel, review of *Philosophy in a New Key*, *Journal of Philosophy* 40 (1943): 323–9.
3 Susanne Langer, *Problems of Art* (New York: Scribner's, 1957), p. 126.
4 Arthur Danto, "The Artworld," *Journal of Philosophy* 61 (1964): 571–84.
5 Arthur Danto, "Artworks and Real Things," *Theoria* 39 (1973): 1–17; "The Transfiguration of the Commonplace," *The Journal of Aesthetics and Art Criticism* 33 (1974): 139–48.
6 Arthur Danto, *The Transfiguration of the Commonplace* (Cambridge, Mass., Harvard University Press, 1981), p. 212.
7 Arthur Danto, "Artworks and Real Things," *Theoria* 39 (1973): 15.
8 See Noël Carroll's "Essence, Expression, and History," in *Danto and his Critics*, ed. Mark Rollins (Cambridge, MA, Blackwell, 1993), pp. 99–100, for a specification of the element of Danto's later theory.
9 George Dickie, "Defining Art," *The American Philosophical Quarterly* 61 (1969): 253–6.
10 George Dickie, *The Art Circle* (New York: Haven, 1984), p. 80.

11 Stephen Davies, *Definitions of Art* (Ithaca, New York: Cornell University Press, 1991), pp. 243. For an extended account of Davies's view see my "Art: Function or Procedure – Nature or Culture?" Ibid., pp. 21–2.

12 Jerrold Levinson, "Extending Art Historically," *The Journal of Aesthetics and Art Criticism* 51 (1993): 411. For a more extended account of Levinson's view see my "Art: Function or Procedure – Nature or Culture?" *The Journal of Aesthetics and Art Criticism* 55 (1993): 22–4.

2

Methodological Background of the Philosophy of Art

I

Philosophical theorizing arose, at least in the West, in ancient Greek times. There and then, the two main competitors for explaining the order that we experience were the atomists and the platonists. The atomists explained this order as being the *result* of the micro-structure of individual things – gold has a different micro-structure from iron, tigers from lions, and so on. The atomists were theorizing about the essence of things, and they did so by talking about spatio-temporal, physical micro-structures. The platonists also explained the order that we experience in the world, but they said that individual things fall into the types that they do because they *participate* in various Forms, these being nonspatial, nontemporal abstractions. The essence of things resides, for the platonists, in the Forms. The atomists and the platonists differed about the nature of the essences of things. They also differed about how the essences are responsible for the order we experience: for the atomists, *causality*[1] was responsible, whereas for the platonists it was *participation*.[2] Thus, at the very beginning of theorizing there was a radical disagreement over what the theorizing was about – about what is *real*.

Once the atomists had enunciated their thesis that the micro-structures of things differ from one another, they then had little else to say about those structures. They spoke of invisible micro-structures but had no means of knowing anything about these essences, although they did speculate about the movement and weight of atoms. They were so far ahead of their times that they were largely speechless; they were barred from inquiry into what they regarded as real by a lack of technology and developed theory.

The platonists, however, were able to speak volumes, for in addition to theorizing about the order and essence of things, they also focused on words and their meanings, which were available in great supply. They had a philosophy of language, which the atomists lacked. The atomists were as speechless about words as they were about invisible micro-structures. The platonists spoke of nonvisible things too, but they claimed we could know them because we understand the words whose meanings were constituted by the nonvisible Forms. The Forms were thus alleged to be not only responsible for the order of things but also were the meanings of words. The knowing of a Form is allegedly demonstrated when a word is understood. Complete knowing of a Form is supposedly demonstrated when an adequate definition of a word – 'figure,' 'justice,' or the like – is successfully achieved.

The voluble platonists with a philosophy of language integrated with and underwritten by their metaphysics won an easy victory over the speechless atomists for control of subsequent philosophizing. Theorizing about the essences of things and the definitions of words – including art and 'art' – thus had its development within the platonic vision of language and reality with reality being understood to be a hierarchically-ordered, rational structure of nonspatial, nontemporal Forms that give order to the world of experience and constitute the intensions of words in a language. The metaphysical structure is rational in the sense that it has the form that would be given by a rational arranger, although no arranger is envisaged within the system. The structure of the Forms is taken to be such that there is a genus/species relation inherent in every intension. Within this vision, the essences of all sorts of different things – gold, water, tigers, justice, art, whatever – are taken to be of the same sort and the essences themselves are subject to dialectical analysis that can yield the intensions – necessary and sufficient conditions – of the words that apply to the things with the essences. For the platonists, inquiry about what is real was conceived of as a search into the intelligible realm of the Forms for essences and meanings or intensions; empirical inquiry was regarded as a pursuit into the illusion of sense. The intellectual agenda was thus set by the platonists, and philosophical inquiry became an attempt to produce the essences of things and the intensions of words. Philosophical inquiry continues to have something of a platonic flavor today.

An apparent advantage the platonists' approach has over the atomists' is that while in principle the atomists have a way of explaining physical phenomena, there is no obvious way for them to explain how nonphysical characteristics (linguistic, moral, cultural, and the like) arise from atomic configurations. On the other hand, the platonists' metaphysics and philosophy of language supposedly deals with all kinds of phenomena from physical to moral.

As is well known, in recent times the search for the essences of art and other notions has been challenged by the claim that there are no such essences and that 'art' and other words apply to the things they do in virtue of intensions that take note of the overlapping similarities among those things. This is a challenge to whatever is left of the platonic tradition in philosophy. There are three main difficulties with this untraditional development. First, it is unclear how the similarities are to be specified – how similar do two characteristics have to be to count as linking two works of art under the word 'art' (or any two objects under the same word), and how many such similarities are required to make two objects fall under the word 'art' (or any word)? Second, the reliance on similarities threatens to draw into and collect into the class of art, or any other notion specified in terms of similarities, every object in the universe because, in some way, everything resembles everything else. Third, focusing now only on art, if one tries to contain the collecting tendencies of similarities by specifying that the similarities must be to prior-established works of art, then an infinite regress of prior-established works of art is generated so that there could never have been a first work of art and hence no present works of art. Since there are works of art, the similarity conception as the whole story is wrong and there would have to be some nonsimilarity ur-work or ur-works of art that have priority over "similarity" art. Thus, some kind of nonsimilarity foundation would be required by the similarity view.

The atomists, the platonists, and the similarity theorists all begin by focusing on the order that they note in things: the platonists infer Forms to explain identities in experience and to be the intensions of all kinds of words, which they take to be manifested in genus/species relationships; the atomists infer conclusions about micro-structures to explain identities of physical phenomena in experience but have nothing to say about intensions; and the similarity theorists forego inference and focus solely on experienced similarities out of which they try to construct intensions. I shall not discuss the similarity theories further.

II

Recently, some philosophers of language have tried to work out a way to adapt the insight of the tongue-tied Greek atomists about the essences of things to the problem of the application of words to things. One of the things that has enabled these philosophers to try to do what the atomists could not try to do is that there are now well worked out and accepted theories of the micro-structure of things that were not available to the atomists. In general, this new technique, according to those who advance it, is said to approach the question of the application of words to things through their *extensions* rather than through intensions.[3] This new approach supposedly contrasts sharply with the traditional, platonic-tinged approach to meaning. One begins, using the new approach, with descriptions of features that function more or less like intensions which serve to focus on some group of things (an extension), and then in the cases of natural kinds one discovers or proceeds with the assurances that an essential, underlying property of the members of the group of things (the extension) can be discovered that uniquely picks out the group of things, or some significant subset of the group of things. This underlying property, if discovered or discoverable, is what identifies this kind of thing in all possible worlds in which that kind of thing exists. Some philosophers of art have subsequently tried to apply this new technique to the philosophy of art.

The approach of platonists is a *top-down* approach; for them, the Forms, which function as intensions, are given and complete, so that, for them, intensions come first as ready-made and determine extensions, the members of which are mere appearances. The new philosophers of language, on the other hand, use a *bottom-up* approach; for them, the discovered or discoverable essential property of the members of an extension constitutes its nature.

These philosophers of language begin, not with a discussion of natural kinds, but with a discussion of proper names as *rigid designators*. According to this view, a proper name such as 'Aristotle' is a rigid designator, a rigid designator being something that picks out the same object in all possible worlds where it exists. Also, according to this view, proper names are introduced by a baptism or dubbing, and we track their referents through the world by means of causal historical chains. Proper names, on this view, function by means of reference or extension rather than by intension. We in later generations have come to believe various propositions about Aristotle, and earlier philosophers of language tried to use these beliefs in one way or another as intensions to pick out Aristotle in all possible worlds. Almost all of our beliefs about Aristotle, however, could be false, and the rigid-designator approach avoids using them in any way.

These philosophers of language then go on to apply the rigid-designator approach to words for *natural kinds*. In the case of an element such as gold, various properties such as being yellow, very malleable, and so on served to focus on a group of objects (an extension); it was later discovered that all or many (a significant subset) of the objects have a particular atomic number which then henceforth serves as the essential, underlying property that picks out the group of gold things. Gold's essential property is being the element with the atomic number 79 and this means that gold is identical with the element with the atomic number 79 and that gold is necessarily the element with the atomic number 79. In the case of a compound such as water, the essential, underlying property turns out to be a particular molecular combination of elements, namely, H_2O; thus, water is necessarily H_2O. In the case of a species of plants or animals, the essential, underlying property would perhaps turn out to be something like a particular DNA profile, although in the cases as complex as organisms the nature of the underlying property would probably be very controversial. These underlying properties serve to identify, for example, gold and water in all possible worlds in which there are such substances. In the cases of elements, compounds and species, the essential properties are underlying because they are micro-structures. The discovery of the essences of natural kinds – 'gold,' 'water,' and so on – is approached through extensions. These philosophers of language have advanced the insight of the Greek atomists to a remarkable degree.

III

James Carney attempted to take the insight of the philosophers of language even further by applying the rigid-designator approach to the problem of what has been characterized in the past as the defining of 'art.'[4] For this application to be possible, according to Carney, it must be the case that a paradigm set of objects had been dubbed 'art' and that the dubbers believed that the objects share a universal property that is a *nature* just as all pieces of gold share the nature of having the atomic number 79. And, for Carney, just as gold is necessarily the element with the atomic number 79, art would necessarily be whatever had the universal property. Carney suggests that it is counterintuitive not to have the belief that works of art have such an extension-determining nature. Carney then says:

> It is not unreasonable to suppose that what Danto, Dickie, and others have called the "artworld" is the subclass in a society that determines the universal property and that they rely on theories of art to do this. The art-

world would be analogous to the metallurgists for "gold", and art theories would play a role similar to scientific theories and "gold" in that they would be taken as hypothesizing the extension-determining property of art.[5]

A few lines later Carney writes, "Theories such as the imitation theory or expression theory would be adequate, since they hypothesize a universal property for paradigms."[6]

What Carney is saying is that any art theory that claims that artworks share an essential property, which of course is every traditional art theory except the similarity view, is a candidate for being fitted to the rigid-designator approach. With all the historical theories of art that have been put forth, Carney's final say on the matter has to be hypothetical: "If the paradigms [of art] have a universal property, then there is a way to determine with certainty whether x is art: x is art if x has the universal property."[7]

This hypothetical resolution leaves open the possibility that different universal properties might be determined by different members of the artworld, assuming for the moment an understanding of the artworld as Carney is envisaging it. On Carney's view, this apparent difficulty is resolved because of the nature of the only two possibilities. If a disagreement arises among the members of the artworld over the common nature of artworks, then the members may decide that all the old paradigms of art do not share a single underlying nature and it will turn out that the old paradigms separate into two or more extensions each with its underlying nature and there will be two or more kinds of art. Or, on the other hand, if a disagreement arises within the artworld over the common nature of artworks, say, over whether a new kind of thing is art with one side citing one nature and another side citing another nature as art-determining, the two sides either accept the two-or-more-kinds-of-art solution just discussed or they can agree on one nature and there will be only one kind of art. So, the members of the artworld will either disagree and there will be more than one kind of art, or they will agree and there will be one kind of art.

Carney's view raises three questions. First, can art theories play the kind of role that scientific theories play in connection with the rigid-designator approach to natural kinds? Carney's answer is "Yes, if they assert a claim of a universal property for the paradigms." This answer raises a second question: "Which art theory is analogous to the atomic theory that yields the atomic number 79 for gold, the molecular theory that describes the molecular structure of water, or the biological theory that specifies

DNA profiles or whatever the correct underlying property is for species?" His answer is that it is the art theory (or theories) with the universal property (or properties) determined by the members of the artworld. This answer raises a third question: "Does the artworld function as Carney envisions?" He does not answer the third question other than to say, "it is not unreasonable to suppose" that it does.[8]

Peter Kivy was the first to attack Carney's suggested approach to theorizing about art.[9] Kivy does not comment on Carney's claim about actions of the members of the artworld, focusing solely on his claim of close analogy between art theories and scientific theories. Where Carney sees analogy, Kivy sees disanalogy. We are not prepared, Kivy says, to accept an art theory in the way that we "are prepared to accept a scientific account of the internal structure of a natural kind."[10] Kivy agrees that in the scientific domain there is a history of discovering that earlier theories are false and of their being replaced by new theories and that this bears some resemblance to art theories being replaced by later art theories. But, he says, the succession of scientific theories is different in that it reveals an increasing scope and ability to deal with the data. Such success in the scientific domain inspires a confidence that is not found in theorizing about art by philosophers.

Thomas Leddy was the next to attack Carney's view.[11] He appears to accept Kivy's point about the disanalogy between art theories and scientific theories, but he focuses on a logically prior analogy alleged in Carney's view – his contention that the artworld determines the universal property of art analogously to the way metallurgists determine the nature of gold. Carney begins by talking about artworld members "hypothesizing" about the universal property of art. Leddy notes, however, that it appears to turn out that on Carney's view the members of the artworld supposedly *determine* the nature of art by *deciding on* a universal property. This contrasts sharply with how metallurgists *determine* the nature of gold; they *discover* the universal property of gold.[12] Thus, Leddy uncovers another difference where Carney's view requires similarity.

What of Carney's claim, which neither Kivy or Leddy addresses, that the members of the artworld function to determine (even if it is only by deciding) the nature of art? Carney says that the members of what Danto, I, and others have called the artworld determines the universal property of art. This makes the artworld into something like a legislative body that deliberates and issues directives that are binding on the other members of society. First, it is not indicated who the "others" are, but the accounts that Danto and I have given of the artworld are very different, although this was perhaps not so clear in mid-1970s when Carney published his view as it is now. Carney writes that Danto's statement that "It is the theory that takes it [*Brillo Box*] up into the artworld" means that we can take his statement to imply "that the extension of the term 'art' is determined by the theories of art held by the artworld."[13] Perhaps Danto's account in "The Artworld" can be construed to fit the rigid-designator approach as Carney says, but I do not think this is Danto's view, and I, for one, do not think that the artworld functions as a legislative body.

Richard Wollheim has attributed to me the view of the artworld as legislative body and then has gone on to ridicule the view.[14] This understanding of the institutional theory of art deserves to be ridiculed because there is no reason at all to think that the artworld or any aspect of it acts like a legislative body – with meetings and decisions, and with declarations and proclamations. Fortunately, the view of the artworld that Wollheim attributes to me is not one that I have ever held,[15] although he and a number of other people seem to have thought I did. I have always understood the artworld to be a background for the practice of creating and experiencing art – a background that is an essential part of the practice.

So, there seem to be two strikes against Carney's view – Kivy's and Leddy's – and perhaps a third against his understanding of the nature of the artworld.

I do think the rigid-designator approach can be fitted to the imitation theory of art and to some versions of the expression theory of art, but not because these theories might be held by members of the artworld. The two theories can be fitted to the approach because they are what I have elsewhere called "natural-kind theories."[16] The philosophers who were the proponents of these two theories were attempting to *identify* art with *one, single*, particular kind of human activity – imitating or the expression of emotion – that can quite reasonably be regarded as *natural* or what today would be thought of as hard-wired. Note the parallel here with gold, water, and species. In the case of gold and the other elements, it turned out that there is a fairly small number (something over a hundred) elements, and physicists discovered that each one has *one* distinct atomic number that uniquely picks it out. (Apparently, isotopes can be ignored.) In the case of water and the other compounds, it turned out that there is a very large number of compounds, but even so physicists and chemists discovered that each one has *one* distinct molecular configuration that uniquely picks it out. The case is perhaps similar for species. It is quite reasonable to suppose that some day the now-hidden, underlying nature of the behavior of imitating or expressing of emotion will be discovered by a scientist – some breed of psychologist/biologist. These two ways of acting would be natural-kind behaviors of natural-kind beings. I am speaking here of imitating and expressing as such; how such imitating and expressing are structured and directed and toward what may vary from culture to culture. By the way, these behaviors are not limited to human beings.

Unfortunately for the imitation and expression theories, there is no good reason to think that either of these behaviors is *identical* with art – some works of art are not imitations or expressions of emotion and some imitations and expressions of emotion are not art – which is why the theories have been almost universally rejected. So, although the imitation theory and the expression theory are the sort of theories that could be fitted to the rigid-designator approach because there is reason to think that imitation and the expression of emotion have underlying essences, it would be a mistake to try to do so because those behaviors just do not match up with all our artworks. They are the wrong theories to use.

IV

There is perhaps a way to fit *certain aspects* of the rigid-designator approach to art, namely, to approach through an extension, looking for an underlying property, although not one that functions in all the ways that a property such as being H_2O does. Consider Carney's procedure. His account of the application of the rigid-designator approach to natural kinds can be summarized by picturing the following pairs: *gold/physicists, water/ physicists and chemists,* and *species/molecular biologists.* Carney then tries to use the rigid-designator approach with the specification of the essence of art, pairing *art* and *members of the artworld.* In effect, Kivy and Leddy in different ways point out that Carney's pairing is not analogous to the earlier pairs which all involve *scientists.* In order to extend those aspects of the rigid-designator approach that I wish to use, the second place in the *art/_____* pair should be filled with the name of some kind of scientist. In the above discussion of the fitting of the imitation and expression theories to the rigid-designator approach, the second place in the pair was filled by psychologists/biologists who presumably would focus on the behavior specified by the two old theories of art. But what I am envisaging here is scientists who would focus directly on the art of our culture or other cultures.

Before trying to apply the aspects of the rigid-designator approach I wish to use to the complicated notion of *art*, consider how it might go with a simpler cultural concept. Assume an anthropologist goes to work, say, in the 1920s on a particular South Pacific island culture. In landing on the island, the anthropologist's native translator is drowned, so she must carry out her studies without the benefit of access to the islanders' language. One of her observations is that many people are referred to as *pukas* but not all. She then observes that only males are pukas, although some of them are fat and some skinny, some are short and some tall, and so on. So what is a puka? In her further observing of the social structure of the islanders, our anthropologist discovers that the teenage boys and girls regularly engage in promiscuous sexual behavior without anyone disapproving but that about age sixteen on the day of the summer solstice they are compelled to stop this behavior by everyone in the society. The sixteen year olds then have the option of participating in an elaborated ceremony in which a male and a female are paired and thereafter must maintain a monogamous relation. Those who choose not to participate in the ceremony are thereafter not permitted to engage in sexual activity with a partner without social disapproval. It is the males who do not participate in the ceremony that are thereafter pukas. So, although it was not at first evident to our anthropologist, the "underlying" feature in the case of pukas is the practice of the members of the culture treating a male sixteen years old or older who has refused to participate in the ceremony that regularizes sexual activity among persons over sixteen in a certain fashion. The practice that our anthropologist takes note of is not underlying or hidden in the way that the universal properties of gold, water and species are, but it is not as obvious as the colors of the islanders' clothes either. It takes some observing, inferring, and theorizing to arrive at an understanding of the cultural practice but the practice in a way is transparent. The cultural practice is underlying but there to be taken note of.

When writing down her notes on the island culture, our anthropologist translates 'puka' as 'bachelor.' When at the end of her first year on the island another native translator arrives, he says that the translation is close but incorrect and that there is no exact equivalent for 'puka' in English. Our anthropologist would have discovered the underlying nature of pukas, but she would then have gone on to translate the word 'puka' wrong. American and European societies do not have pukas because we do not compel the ceremony and behavior described above. Any society that did compel the ceremony and behavior described would have pukas, even if only this island in fact had this practice. Pukas are individuals compelled and regulated as described, and they would be such in all possible worlds in which they exist. Our anthropologist would have constructed an essentially correct theory of one aspect of the island culture without the help of the intensional content of the island language, although her use of 'bachelor' in her account is not quite right. Pukas and bachelors are similar in certain central respect, but they also differ in some important central aspects, so we cannot say that they have the same underlying nature.

The underlying nature that bachelors have and the underlying nature that pukas could have, unlike the *physical* reality that gold, water and species have, are *cultural* realities.[17] Such cultural natures are or would be a small part of a larger reality that is constituted by webs of relations that are or could be instituted by a society of persons.

V

Theorizing about art began in and has been carried out throughout almost all of its history in the Platonic mode, which focuses on discovering the intensions of our words. Even when philosophers have given up on Forms, they have continued the *top-down* approach of seeking intensions – in the analysis of concepts, in ordinary language, or in just seeking definitions without saying how they are doing so. The "intensional" approach, which focuses on language, will not work for such terms as 'gold,' 'water' and their like, but it appears to work for terms like 'bachelor.' Carney himself mentions that, unlike 'gold,' 'bachelor' has a specifiable intension. He writes, "A term like 'bachelor' in its accurate adult use is introduced as a synonym for 'adult male not previously married.'"[18] Carney's saying that 'bachelor' is "introduced as a synonym" makes it sound as if the term was put into the language in the way a technical term is introduced by a philosopher or a logician, but of course he does not mean that it was. 'Bachelor' came into the language as a co-relative term to 'marriage' and both terms (and many others) ride on practices that we have instituted as a cultural group. So, 'bachelor,' unlike 'gold,' has an intension, but on the other hand, 'bachelor,' like 'gold, can be approached through its extension. Although in the case of an English word like 'bachelor,' we never bother to do this because, as native speakers of English, we have intensional access to its meaning. In the imagined case of pukas, the language-deprived anthropologist is forced to approach through an extension because she lacks intensional access the islander's language.

The concepts *bachelor* and *puka*, unlike the concepts *gold*, *water* and *tiger*, are transparent, that is, a person who knows the culture in which the concept functions, knows the concept. The natures of bachelors and pukas are underlying in the sense that one cannot just look at an individual and see that he is a bachelor or a puka, one must know whether an individual is enmeshed in the relevant cultural relations.

The nature of bachelors and the nature of gold are similar in that they are discoverable by empirical inquiry. The natures differ in that the nature of bachelors depends on cultural developments – decisions and the like – whereas that of gold does not. So, one is tempted to say that the nature of gold cannot change, which is true, but that the nature of bachelors can, which is misleading. The use of the word 'bachelor' can change in a several different ways. Assume that at a given time the word has one meaning. The word could change its meaning entirely while still having only one meaning. It could change entirely and have two completely new meanings. The word could acquire a second meaning with the original meaning remaining unchanged and so on. But even if the word 'bachelor' changed in one of these ways or even if the word ceased to exist as a word in the language, the condition of being an unmarried adult male and the cultural practice of categorizing such an individual need not change. The condition and practice remains a logical possibility even if 'bachelor' ceases to exist in the language and every person is in fact married or previously married.

I believe the concept *art* is like the concept *bachelor* (and the concept *puka*), and the word 'art' is like the word 'bachelor' (and the word 'puka'). Of course, no one has ever felt the need to put forth a theory of bachelorness. Plato seems never to have felt the need to write a dialogue about it as he did about piety, friendship, and justice or even to attack it in passing as metaphysically inferior and psychologically dangerous as he did art. Why has no one ever felt the need for a theory of bachelorness? Perhaps, because 'bachelor' does not serve as an evaluative weapon-word in the way that 'art' does. And, no doubt for a variety of other reasons, but probably no one has ever felt the need for a theory of bachelorness because intensional access to its meaning is so easy and uncontroversial. In any event, Plato did theorize about art and did attack art on metaphysical and psychological grounds, and philosophers have been trying to theorize about art ever since. Intensional access to 'art' is obviously much more difficult than to 'bachelor,' and it is clearly much more controversial. We do not seem to need to apply what may be called 'the extensional approach' to 'bachelor,' but perhaps the difficulty and controversy involved with 'art' can be avoided by using the extensional approach with it.

Earlier I noted that in order to use the extensional approach to 'art' that the second place in the *art/_____* pair should be filled with the name of some kind of scientist. Following the pattern established with the case of bachelors and pukas, I think the pair should be *art/cultural anthropologists*. Art is, I have long believed, a cultural notion, and cultural anthropologists are the scientists that deal with cultural phenomena. My own belief in art as a cultural phenomenon is demonstrated by the fact that the institutional theory of art, which I have been defending in one form or another for a long time, is clearly a cultural theory. Perhaps it is worth noting that Leddy twice alludes to art as a cultural concept by contrasting it with what he calls natural science concepts in his 1987 article that I discussed above but that is all he says on the topic.

When I say that art is a cultural notion, I mean that it is a phenomenon that has been invented by a cultural group and that it is not a genetically determined behavior like mating, eating, and the like.[19] In saying this, I do not mean to suggest that only we or some small group of societies have art or our concept of *art*. I think that Dennis Dutton is probably right that all human societies have art.[20] Of course, there could be and might be a human society that does not yet in fact have art. I only wish to say of each society that has art that it was invented at some point in the past. It is, of course, possible that in the case of a given society that art was imported from another culture before it could be invented indigenously, so in this case the point in the past referred to would be in the past of another society.

What would be the general features of the application of the extensional approach to the notion of art using the *art/cultural anthropologist* pairing? We would be looking for a cultural phenomenon that is shared by all cultures or at least many cultures, since, as noted, a given culture might not yet have art. The phenomenon would have to be of a cultural nature that is the same in all cultures that have it. That nature would have to be of a rather abstract kind, given the widely differing kinds of art that there are. And, it might be that there are things that very closely resemble a kind of art that are not art; that is, there could be an arbitrariness about one thing's being art and a very closely resembling thing not being art. Such arbitrariness is perhaps inevitable where cultural matters are concerned, because cultural matters are how they are as the result of how a culture has 'set things up' at some time or during some period in the past.

It would perhaps be best to begin our looking within our own culture. We would approach our own culture as the imagined anthropologist did the island culture, except that we have the advantage that we are native speakers of our own language. Of course, various aspects of language could be handicaps that leads native speakers astray. Words in their dictionary senses typically have a number of different meanings, which could be confusing. Further, we (and any native speaker of any natural language) can make a word mean a large number of different things by the use of inflection, irony, gestures, juxtaposition, and the like and this too may confuse us in the cases of the meanings of some words. All of this linguistic flexibility may obscure our view of the *practices* that underlie the specific meanings of some words. We might be better able to isolate these specific meanings of these practice-dependent words if we were language-deprived observers, like the imagined anthropologist. Of course, language-deprived observers can make the kind of mistranslation imagined.

The first lesson to be derived from the imagined case of the language-deprived anthropologist's mistranslation is that in the case of the meaning of culturally determined words, access to the intensional content of the language of the members of the culture involved can be useful. The second lesson to be derived from the case of the language-deprived anthropologist (one ignored by the purely intensional approaches of historical philosophers of art) is that in the cases of certain concepts and the words that go with them, knowledge of the practices that underlie the concepts and their words is crucial to their meaning. Applying these two lessons, it may be possible to make some progress in theorizing about art.

To apply the extensional approach to the notion of art using the *art/ cultural anthropologist* pairing, one needs to look for linguistic usage that is integrated with cultural practice analogous to the islanders' use of 'puka' and their practice involved in organizing the cultural activities of pukas, and our use of 'bachelor' and the practice involved in our organizing the cultural practice of bachelors.

If we start, as cultural anthropologists, with our own linguistic usage, the usages of 'art' would have to relate to a provisional description in the way that the usages of 'gold' relate to the properties of being yellow and malleable as a provisional description. In the way that physicists then focus on yellow and malleable objects on their way to discovering the atomic number of gold, cultural anthropologists will have to start by focusing on objects that satisfy the provisional description. The usages we will find with 'art,' however, because of our wide linguistic flexibility, will be all over the place. But note that the usages of 'gold' will be too; consider, "You struck gold!" said to someone who bought Xerox stock early on or to the discoverer of an important scientific truth. Despite all of its many and varied usages, with 'gold' we somehow winnowed our way down to a preliminary extension of yellow and malleable objects and then proceeded to atomic theorizing. With 'art,' we will have to winnow our way down to a reasonable preliminary extension and then look for a cultural practice that underlies this preliminary extension or some significant subset of it.

We can think of the history of the philosophy of art – from Plato to Danto – as a kind of winnowing of the preliminary description of 'work of art,' although, as we shall see, the process does not always eliminate items from the extension of works of art – sometimes it adds them.

Not even the earliest imitation theorist would have been moved to think of driftwood as art if some other ancient Greek, foreshadowing Morris Weitz and some other twentieth-century philosophers, had uttered the Greek equivalent of 'That driftwood is a lovely piece of sculpture.' He would not have considered the driftwood to be within the extension of art, not only because it is not an imitation but also because it is not an artifact, that is, a human creation. Someone has to be in the grip of a philosophical movement to think that a piece of driftwood all by itself is an artwork because it has been referred to as a lovely piece of sculpture. Thus, nonartifactuality was winnowed out of (or perhaps it should be said never got into) the preliminary description of 'work of art' by virtue of something like common sense.

Imitation theorists were, however, moved – eventually anyway – by another kind of case: things that were obviously not imitations but which seemed like artworks nevertheless. Being bothered by this kind of case forced an expansion in their conception of the intension of artworks and caused them to cease being imitation theorists. The expansion of the intension of artworks by counterexamples advanced by others or just noticed has been a standard feature of theorizing about art. Notice that to work as a counterexample to someone's theory, the alleged counterexample must plausibly fit into an extension *despite* the fact that it lacks all or some part of the theorist's understanding of the intension of a term under consideration. This kind of philosophical move has been responsible, not for a winnowing out of characteristics from the preliminary description of 'work of art,' but for an adding of characteristics. This kind of move eliminates theories – the imitation theory of art, for example, and, I think, the expression theory as well.

I think that virtually all philosophers of art – present and past – are and always have been agreed that it is poems, painting, plays, sonatas, sculptures, and such familiar items that are works of art and that this is the extension that they are and always have been theorizing about – trying to state the intension that fits it. There has of course been some disagreement as to whether to count dada objects and similar things as works of art, but this is a skirmish of little significance. I have maintained that dada objects are theoretically useful because they have helped us gain insight into the art-making context in which works of art are embedded either because dada objects are works of art or because they are not works of art but have been mistaken for works of art by some people. In any event, let us set aside this dispute and focus attention on the huge group of works of art about which there is complete agreement.

The philosophical problem with the large group of items that constitutes the extension of works of art has always been the great diversity of its members. This heterogeneousness has been the great barrier to the traditional attempts to extract the intension from the exhibited features[21] of these works. By 'exhibited features' I mean characteristics that can be noticed by directly experiencing works of art – for example, that they are representations, are expressive, are delicate, and the like. What exhibited features could be found to be exemplified in all these many and diverse works of art? And what a ready source of counterexamples that same diversity has been against all those imitationists, expressionists, and the like who have tried to specify partial or complete conditions from among exhibited features.

Focus now on present-day theories of art. I think Danto's attempt to characterize art in terms of *aboutness* is an example of the traditional search for the intensional meaning of 'work of art' among exhibited characteristics, and I believe that his theory is vulnerable to the traditional kind of counterexample attack.[22] Beardsley's attempt to characterize art in terms of aesthetic character is also an example of the same traditional search among exhibited characteristics and is subject to the same kind of attack.[23] On the other hand, I think Jerrold Levinson's historical theory and my institutional theory are different from the traditional theories and can be understood as attempts to discover the underlying nature of the extension of works of art – the underlying nature being the *nonexhibited* feature of works of art that ties them together. I will not discuss Levinson's theory here because I have discussed its difficulties elsewhere.[24]

What would a search by a cultural anthropologist uncover in a study of the 'how we deal with' works of art? I believe such a search would reveal an underlying cultural structure like that envisaged by the institutional theory of art. The institutional theory is an account of the cultural structure within which works of art are produced and function, and the structure itself is specified in terms of a variety of cultural roles.

In any event, even if cultural anthropologists could not find a cultural structure identical with that described by the institutional theory, I believe they would find a structure very much like it. That is, they would find a structure of the general sort that the five declarations I gave as definitions in *The Art Circle* can serve as a summary account of. These five are as follows:

1   An artist is a person who participates with understanding in the making of a work of art.
2   A work of art is an artifact of a kind created to be presented to an artworld public.
3   A public is a set of persons the members of which are prepared in some degree to understand an object which is presented to them.
4   The artworld is the totality of all artworld systems.
5   An artworld system is a framework for the presentation of a work of art by an artist to an artworld public.[25]

The structure presented by these five would be the sort of thing that constitutes the cultural essence of the institution within which art has its being. And, the second declaration (definition) is the sort of thing that can be taken as a statement of the cultural essence of a work of art, namely, a statement that identifies art with the complicated property of being an artifact of a kind created to be presented to an artworld public.

VI

Assume for argument's sake that 'A work of art is an artifact of a kind created to be presented to an artworld public' captures the cultural essence of art because the statement has been arrived at by means of a search by anthropologists into cultural structure. Would that mean that it states the intension of 'work of art'? When Carney applies the rigid-designator approach to 'work of art,' he concludes that 'work of art' has no intension. Remember, however, what Carney says about 'bachelor,' namely, that it has an intension. So, Carney treats words like 'bachelor' differently from the way in which he treats words like 'gold.' He does not explain why 'bachelor' is different from 'gold,' and there is nothing in his article that requires him to do so. I, however, have claimed that what I am calling 'the extensional approach' can be applied to 'work of art' and have also tried to apply it to 'bachelor' as well. So, I need at least to show how 'bachelor' has an intension if the extensional approach can be applied to it.

In effect, I have agreed with Carney that 'bachelor' *means* 'an adult male not previously married' and added that *being* an adult male not previously married is the underlying *cultural* nature of bachelors. How does the case of the nature of bachelors, which is derived by means of the extensional approach, differ from that of the nature of gold, which is derived by means of the rigid-designator approach? And, how does the case of 'bachelor' differ from 'gold' so that 'bachelor' can have an intension and 'gold' does not?

First, consider the question of how the nature of bachelors differs from the nature of gold. First, the nature of bachelors is a cultural nature; it is a cultural status. Being a bachelor is of course not a legal status, but it is related to and derived from marriage, which is a matter of law – law being an officially enacted cultural phenomenon. Marriage is a cultural (legal) way of organizing various central aspect of the lives of human beings. Being a bachelor is a cultural (nonlegal) way of organizing aspects of lives of some human males – how and under what circumstances, for example, certain human males are invited to dinner. The nature of gold, on the other hand, is not cultural, but physical. There would be gold if there were no cultures anywhere. There could not be bachelors without a culture and in fact not without a culture that has marriage. We have no control over the nature of gold, but we do have control over the nature of cultural things, although it is a complicated matter.

There is another important difference between the nature of gold and the nature of bachelors. An individual sample of gold in the actual world (the element with the atomic number 79) would be gold in all possible worlds, that is, the individual sample of gold is necessarily the element with the atomic number 79. In contrast, an individual bachelor Adam in the actual world might be a married man in some possible worlds and thus not a bachelor in all possible worlds, that is, the individual bachelor Adam is not necessarily a bachelor. Being gold is a nature that might be called an intrinsic nature, while being a bachelor is a nature that an individual acquires by fitting into a cultural context. It is worth noting in passing that particular works of art are like bachelors in this respect. For example, a particular physical object that is a work of representational art in the actual world might not be a work of art in some possible world because that possible world lacks the cultural institution of art and that particular physical object would then merely be a representation; thus, a particular work of art in the actual world is not necessarily a work of art.

Second, in the case of discovering (or just knowing) the nature of bachelors, there is no intellectual division of labor that requires experts to discover that nature as is required in the case of gold. Gold has a hidden nature that requires highly specialized individuals – physicists, chemists, and the like – to discover its nature. The nature of bachelors, although it is underlying in being a culturally founded phenomenon, is known to virtually everyone; its nature is transparent rather than hidden.

Consider now how 'bachelor' differs from 'gold.' First, 'bachelor' is a cultural term in that it derives in part from the cultural term 'married,' although of course it also involves the biological terms 'adult' (which may be given some cultural content by way of a roughly specified age designation) and male. Gold is not a cultural term but a physical term, that is, it refers to objects with a physical nature.

Second, 'bachelor' has some similarity to technical words that are stipulated to have a certain meaning. In the case of technical terms, it is typically individual persons who do the stipulating, but in the case of words like 'bachelor,' it is the culture that does the 'stipulating' or something like stipulating that may be called cultural determination. The exact nature of this determination is vague, and furthermore the courses of the various determinations probably differ in the cases of different cultural terms. The cultural determination of the meaning of cultural words is of course closely related to the fact that we have some control over the natures of cultural matters.

There is an intimate connection between 'bachelor' and the nature of bachelors – a sort of congruency in which the intension of 'bachelor' and the nature of the members of the extension of 'bachelor' are determined by our culture in a logically concomitant way. The word 'bachelor' (and its definition) and the nature of bachelors are both the same kind of thing, namely, they are both cultural products. Both are coordinated and mirroring products of how we organize the intertwined pathways of our linguistic and behavioral lives. 'Gold' and the nature of gold lack this intimate, mirroring relationship. We are participants in the initiating and maintaining of the cultural natures of the kinds of things of which being a bachelor is a prime example; these are cultural kinds. In contrast, we have no such 'insider' relation to the natures of natural kinds.

The inarticulate Greek atomists were on the right track about gold. In a way, the platonists would have been on the right track if they had turned their attention to transparent terms like 'bachelor'; they would have had, however, to focus attention, not on rational intuition of Forms in which supposedly every sort of thing participates, but on the understanding of our participation in cultural practices that are involved with transparent terms.

The cultural term 'work of art' is, I believe, like the cultural term 'bachelor' and not like the physical term 'gold.' There is an intimate cultural connection between "work of art" and the nature of a work of art that our cultural anthropologists can discover such that that nature can be converted into a definition of 'work of art.' I hope it will be discovered that the definition is my institutional one.

Notes

I wish to thank Suzanne Cunningham and Ruth Marcus for reading and commenting on earlier versions of this chapter.

1   In ancient Greek times perhaps this would have been called efficient causality.
2   In ancient Greek times this might have been called formal causality.
3   This approach is derived from the well-known work of Saul Kripke and Hilary Putnam.
4   James Carney, "Defining Art," *British Journal of Aesthetics* 15 (1975): 191–206 and "A Kripkean Approach to Aesthetic Theories," *British Journal of Aesthetics* 22 (1982): 150–7.
5   Ibid., "Defining Art," p. 200.
6   Ibid., p. 201.
7   Ibid., p. 200.
8   Ibid., p. 200.
9   Peter Kivy, "Aesthetic Concepts: Some Fresh Considerations," *The Journal of Aesthetics and Art Criticism* 37 (1979): 423–32.
10   Ibid., p. 430.
11   Thomas Leddy, "Rigid Designation in Defining Art," *The Journal of Aesthetics and Art Criticism* 45 (1987): 263–72.
12   Ibid., p. 264.
13   Ibid., "Defining Art," p. 201.
14   Richard Wollheim, *Painting as an Art* (NJ: Princeton University Press, 1987), pp. 14–15.
15   See George Dickie, "An Artistic Misunderstanding," *The Journal of Aesthetics and Art Criticism* 51 (1993): 69–71.
16   George Dickie, "Art: Function or Procedure – Nature or Culture?," *The Journal of Aesthetics and Art Criticism* 55 (1997): pp. 25–8.

17 See John Searle, *The Construction of Social Reality* (Simon & Schuster, New York, 1997).

18 Carney, "Defining Art," p. 199.

19 For a discussion of cultural-kind and natural-kind theories of art, see Dickie, "Art: Function or Procedure – Nature or Culture?," pp. 25–8.

20 Dennis Dutton, "But They Don't Have Our Concept of Art," in *Theories of Art Today*, ed. Noël Carroll (University of Wisconsin Press, 2000) pp. 217–38.

21 The distinction between the exhibited and nonexhibited features of works of art was first made and used by Maurice Mandelbaum in his "Family Resemblances and Generalization Concerning the Arts," *American Philosophical Quarterly* 2 (1965): 219–28.

22 See my "Tale of Two Artworlds," in *Danto and His Critics*, ed. Mark Rollins (Oxford: Blackwell Publishers, 1993) pp. 76–7 and Noël Carroll, "Essence, Expression, and History," ibid., pp. 79–106.

23 Monroe Beardsley, "In Defense of Aesthetic Value," *Proceedings and Addresses of the American Philosophical Association* (Newark, Del.: American Philosophical Association, 1979), p. 729; Monroe Beardsley, "Redefining Art," *The Aesthetic Point of View: Selected Essays*, ed. M. J. Wreen and D. M. Callen (Cornell University Press), p. 299.

24 See Dickie, "Art: Function or Procedure – Nature or Culture," pp. 22–4.

25 George Dickie, *The Art Circle* (Evanston, Il.: Chicago Spectrum Press, 1997), pp. 80–2. Originally published in 1984.

3

Nature of Art Theories

In his 1991 book, *Definitions of Art*,[1] Stephen Davies devotes the bulk of its space to categorizing and considering twentieth-century theories of art produced since 1964 under the headings of *functional* and *procedural*. Near the end of his book he introduces a third category of art theories – the *historical* – and discusses several such theories. In the first part of this chapter, I shall discuss most of these same theories in terms of Davies's categories and in the light of his analyses and criticisms. While I accept a great deal of what Davies says about these theories, I will take issue with some of his most important conclusions. In the second part of the chapter, I shall introduce an alternative way of classifying the theories and/or the aspects of theories Davies discusses, which uses the notions of natural-kind theories of art and cultural-kind theories of art that were discussed in chapter 2. I shall not be claiming this alternative way is a better one than Davies's, just that it is a different way of classifying and that it throws a different light on these theories.

I

From ancient times to the present day, the great bulk of the theories of art have been functional, i.e., theories that define 'art' in terms of what is taken to be art's essential function or functions. As Davies puts it, these theories are concerned with the point or points of art as defining. Since Davies does not consider *any* theories produced before 1964, there are many well-known, twentieth-century, *functional* theories of art that he does not discuss. R. G. Collingwood's view that art is the expression of emotion is a good example of such a pre-1964 functional theory. According to Collingwood, the essential function or point of art is to express emotion. Susanne Langer's definition of art as "the creation of forms symbolic of human feeling" is another example of a pre-1964 functional theory; the point of art, according to Langer, is to symbolize (actually resemble) human feeling. Many other examples could be cited. Before 1964, virtually all theories of art were functional, but after that year a new kind of art theory became possible.

Despite the multipicity of twentieth-century functional theories, Davies discusses only Monroe Beardsley's functional view of the nature of art, which he subjects to an extensive review and criticism. Beardsley produced the first version of his theory in 1979, a date late in his career and a date well after what Davies calls "procedural theories" had begun to appear. In addition to setting forth his view as the correct view, I think Beardsley presented his theory as an attempt to stem the tide of procedural theories initiated in 1964 by Arthur Danto's "The Artworld." Beardsley formulated several versions of his functional definition, but his first is the simplest and most straightforward. He wrote, "an artwork can be usefully defined as an intentional arrangement of conditions for affording experiences with marked aesthetic character."[2] For Beardsley, the essential function of art is the capacity to produce aesthetic experience. I shall not discuss Beardsley's view because I accept Davies's criticisms and rejection of it and because I have discussed Beardsley's theory on so many other occasions, most notably in chapter IV of the *The Art Circle*.[3]

The procedural account to which Davies devotes his almost undivided attention is my institutional theory of art. The title of the chapter in which the main discussion of proceduralism occurs is entitled, "Dickie's Institutional Theory of the Definition of Art."[4] At the beginning of this chapter, Davies devotes several pages to Danto's writings on the philosophy of art. He treats Danto's writings on this topic as the presentation of a *single* theory and concludes that Danto's view is compatible with, although not identical with, the institutional approach. I think things are more complicated than Davies thinks and that there are two distinct theories set forth in Danto's writings – the early view of "The Artworld" and an almost entirely different view presented in his work after "The Artworld." The classification of Danto's theories in terms of the functional/procedural distinction is more complicated than Davies thinks.

"The Artworld" introduced a new way of thinking into the philosophy of art by the use of an argument that can be called "The Perceptually-Indistinguishable-Objects Argument," and Danto continued to use this argument and ones similar to it in his later writings. The argument, as it applies to visual art, goes as follows. Consider a pair of visually indistinguishable objects, either an actual pair such as *Fountain* and a urinal that exactly resembles it or a pair such as the actual painting *The Polish Rider* and a thought-experiment object – an accidently produced paint-on-canvas object that exactly resembles *The Polish Rider*. Either pair suffices for the argument. In such a pair, one object is a work of art and the other is not or would not be an artwork, and since they exactly resemble one another, it cannot be some visually discernible characteristic that makes the artwork art. Therefore, it must be some context involving at least some nonvisble elements that makes the artwork art. The conclusion Danto draws in "The Artworld" is that it is a specific kind of context in which something is embedded that makes it art, not something it functions to do. The way in which he specifies the context can be seen from the following quotations from "The Artworld."

> What in the end makes the difference between a Brillo Box and a work of art consisting of a Brillo Box is a certain theory of art. It is the theory that takes it up into the world of art. . . .

> It is the role of artistic theories, these days as always, to make the artworld, and art, possible.

> It would, I should think, never have occurred to the painters of Lascaux that they were producing *art* on those walls. Not unless there were neolithic aestheticians.[5]

In the last quoted passage I take Danto to be saying that the Lascaux painters were not producing art and that this is so because there were no neolithic aestheticians to produce art theories to make art possible. In these passages, Danto is claiming that art theories are either necessary and sufficient or at least necessary for art to be created.

It is plausible that dadaist works and Warhol-like works were made possible by their creators antecedently having an art theory or at least theoretical thoughts about art in mind. Danto, however, says that this is true not only for such unusual and recent works but that "it is the role of artistic theories . . . *as always* . . . to make art possible" (italic mine). And, he thinks that the lack of artistic theories (neolithic or otherwise) makes art impossible.

It has always seemed to me that Danto's view cannot be right because art was being produced long before ancient Greece began producing philosophers and any theory of art. Independently of its truth, Danto's theory is important because it was the first procedural theory. This theory is, given Davies's categories, a procedural one, since according to it, something is art, not because of what it functions to do, but because of the place it comes to occupy within an art-specific context; that is, something is art because an "[art] theory takes it up into the world of art. . . ." A pre-existing art theory's "taking up into" is a kind of procedure that something undergoes that is responsible for its arthood.

Later, in 1973[6] and 1974,[7] Danto began claiming that being *about* something is a necessary condition of art. In his 1981 book, Danto amplified his view into a full-blown theory of art.[8] This later theory, which revolves around *aboutness*, represents a radical, although not total, break with the view of "The Artworld." On Noël Carroll's account of the later theory as presented in Danto's book, which Danto agrees is accurate, it is specified that a work of art is (1) about something, (2) projects a point-of-view (3) by means of rhetorical ellipsis, (4) requires interpretation, and that (5) the work and interpretation requires an art historical context.[9] The first four items appear to be an expansion of the earlier aboutness thesis, while the fifth item, which involves art historical contexts, appears to hark back to the even earlier "The Artworld."

In 1973, Danto wrote that "art *is* a language of sorts"[10] and the first four items that Carroll discriminates in Danto's later theory fits within the language domain. The final requirement of an art historical context is distinct from the linguistic aspect of the theory. Danto's post-1973 theory is more difficult to classify than the earlier procedural one. The four aboutness items incline the theory in the direction of functionalism – it is a necessary condition of art to be *about* something. The art historical context requirement inclines the theory in the direction of proceduralism – it is necessary for an artwork to hold a place in an art historical succession. With regard to the functional/procedural distinction, Danto's later theory appears to be a mixed one. I am, by the way, not claiming that there is something wrong with his theory because it is mixed in this way.

The greatest difficulty with Danto's later theory is that, although there are many, many artworks that are about something, there are also many, many artworks that are not about anything. I have repeatedly raised this point, as have others, about the large number of apparent counterexamples to Danto's later theory. Danto's response to this criticism is to claim that artworks such as nonobjective art that appear not to be about anything are about art. Certainly some nonobjective artworks are about art but I do not think that all are. In 2000, Danto is still defending the aboutness of art by saying that he can show that any actual painting alleged to be a counterexample to the aboutness of art is actually about something. In support of his claim, he gives a set of examples. He writes, "Sean Scully's paintings are composed chiefly of stripes, but they are meant to assert propositions about human life, about love, about, even, death"[11] How an artist's intention can make stripes be about life, love, or death Danto does not say, and I do not see how it could. The stripes on the flag of the United States are about something, but this is a different kind of case entirely because not only are the stripes meant to be about something, they are widely understood to mean something and have been so understood for a very long time.

Why does Danto insist on the necessity of aboutness for art when it seems so obvious that many works of art are not about anything? The answer is to be found, I think, not in what he says about art when he talks about the philosophy of art but in what he understands philosophy to be when he talks about the philosophy of art. Early in his book, *The Transfiguration of the Commonplace*, he writes:

> For me, in many ways the paradigm of a philosophical theory is what we find in the [Wittgenstein's] *Tractatus*, where a contrast is drawn between the world, on the one side, and its mirror image in discourse on the other. . . . It is a theory full of problems and obscurities, . . . but I am interested in enlisting it solely as the *form* of a philosophical theory, all the more because what is philosophical about it is the picture it presents of the relationship between language and the world. . . .[12]

For Danto, in order for a theory to be a philosophical theory, it has to be about the relationship between language and the world. So, for him, in order for a theory to be a philosophical theory of art, that is, a philosphy of art, it must fall into the category of theories that are about language's relationship to the world. When Danto focuses on the phrase "philosophy of art," he attends solely to the word "philosophy" and forces art to submit to it. I think this reverses the proper method of the philosophy of art which is to focus first on works of art to see if they have any universal characteristics that it is reasonable to take as necessary. Danto's equating of philosophy and ontology has unfortuate implications not only for the philosphy of art but for any philosophical endeavor that does not fit easily into the role of investigating language's power to describe the world.

As noted earlier, the chapter that Davies devotes to the discusssion of the procedural theory of art is entitled "Dickie's Institutional Theory of the Definition of Art." This title, however, is misleading. Although Davies quotes the early version of the definition of "work of art" from *Art and the Aesthetic* and the later version's definitions of "artist," "work of art," "public," "artworld," and "artworld system" from *The Art Circle*, he does not, as he himself notes, discuss in any detail either of my versions of the theory. He is primarily interested in the general institutional approach, an approach that he endorses. Davies, nevertheless, makes no attempt to work out his own institutional theory, he just notes what he regards as some central features of such a view.

Davies rejects both of my versions of the institutional theory because both lack what he takes to be a necessary ingredient of institutionalism – the notion of *the conferring of the status of art*. Although he has something to say about this ingredient, he never really justifies its necessity for institutionalism.

Davies is right that both of my versions lack what he takes to be the necessary feature, although in *Art and the Aesthetic* I did sometimes carelessly write of conferring *the status of art*. The official view of this earlier book, however, is that candidacy of appreciation is conferred and artifactuality may sometimes be conferred. Davies appears to think more highly of the earlier version, presumably because it at least speaks about conferring something and the later version does not.

Davies's evaluation of my versions of the institutional theory are summed up in the following two quotations from his book.

> Dickie too often discusses the conferral of art status as if it were a kind of action, like shaving, rather than an exercise of authority vested in socially defined roles, with the result that he has no useful explanation to offer of who can confer art status on what and when.[13]

> An artist is someone who has acquired (in some appropriate but informal fashion) the authority to confer status. By "authority" I do not mean "a right to others' obedience"; I mean an "entitlement successfully to employ the conventions by which art status is conferred on objects/events."[14]

Davies thinks that the necessary feature of conferring the status of art in turn rests on an exercise of authority by an artist.

One problem that Davies thinks will be solved by his notion of authority is the circularity of my versions of the institutional theory, although it is not very clear to me how this would be accomplished. Since I do not regard circularity to be a problem and because I discussed this point at length in *The Art Circle*, I shall not pursue this matter here.[15]

I have of course never held that art status is conferred, but Davies thinks that I and any institutionalist should. Moreover, he thinks that the creation of art derives from an act of authority. He contrasts the authority that Duchamp allegedly exercised in creating *Fountain* with the lack of authority of the plumbing salesman I imagined in *Art and the Aesthetic*. I claimed such a salesman could have done what Duchamp did if he had the imagination and wit to do so. Davies's view is that art is created by an exercise of authority – an exercise of an entitlement to employ art-making conventions. He claims that my imaginary plumbing salesman would lack such authority. Davies never gives any argument in support of his claim. Is his claim true?

Consider a mundane example of art creation. An artist paints away in his studio on a canvas and after a while says to himself, "It's finished," and he then signs the painting. A work of art has been created but there has been no exercise of authority that is *responsible for* its creation. The artist may have exercised some skill, imagination, knowledge of a particular sort, and the like. Neither our artist nor Duchamp exercises authority in creating art. After the fact of art creation, an artist may exercise authority over his paintings because they are his or her property – for example, authorize a gallery owner to display them for sale. Perhaps Duchamp exercised such after-the-fact-of-art-creation authority in getting *Fountain* displayed at that now famous art show. An artist also exercises a similar authority of the property sort when he or she says, "It is finished," but having the authority to determine when one's own work is completed is not at all the kind of authority Davies has in mind. For Davies, the relevant authority is the authority to exercise an entitlement to employ art-making conventions.[16]

I think one can be in a position to do something because possessed of authority or in a position to do something for other reasons. A policeman, a doctor, a pharmacist, a parent, and the like are in a position to do certain things because they have the authority to do them that is acquired within a legal system. But one can be in a position to do something, not because of authority, but because of knowledge and skill. Someone might be in a position to do CPR or the Heimlich maneuver simply because of the knowledge of how to do them. One does not have to have authority to do such things. On the other hand, to write an order for a prescription drug one must possess certain medical authority and be licensed by the state to have the legal authority to do so. I think that the creation of art falls under the notion of being in a position to do something because of the possession of knowledge (and sometimes skill). The general conceptual scheme I have in mind is this. There is the more general notion of being in a position to do something. Under this general notion there are two species: (1) being in a position to do something because of authority, and (2) being in a position to do something independently of authority.

In a review of *Definitions of Art*, Ira Newman makes a similar point about Davies's notion of authority. Newman writes:

> By invoking the notion of authority and roles, Davies has a political or organizational structure in mind. . . . So Davies' notion [of authority] has to be viewed as, at best, metaphorical: that is, it is *as if* the members of the artworld conferred art status the way ministers and judges do. Yet Davies offers few supporting reasons for viewing this metaphor as an apt one. There is nothing remotely like a process of election or selection in which members of the artworld assume posts for conferring artwork status. And knowledge of art's history and theory (so central to understanding why Duchamp's *Fountain* may be an artwork) does not achieve anything like granting the authority to *bestow* art status; . . . this is the "authority" of a qualified expert, and an altogether different sense from the one Davies has in mind. Davies' notion of authority thus seems as mysterious, at this stage, as the concepts it is intended to illuminate.[17]

I conclude that Davies main objections to my versions of institutionalism, namely, that both lack an account of how art status is conferred and how it is conferred by an exercise of authority, are unfounded.

I turn now from functional and procedural theories of art to which Davies devotes so much attention to a discussion of two of the historical theories Davies treats – Jerrold Levinson's, to which Davies devotes considerable space, and Noël Carroll's, to which he discusses briefly.

In 1979, Levinson offers what Davies calls an "historical/intentional" definition of "art," which Levinson presented as inspired by the institutional theory.[18] He, however, offers his theory as a competitor to the institutional view. Levinson gave the following definition:

> X is an artwork at t = df X is an object of which it is true at t that some person or persons, having the appropriate proprietary right over X, non-passingly intends (or intended) X for regard-as-a-work-of-art, i.e., regard in any way (or ways) in which objects in the extension of "art work" prior to t are or were correctly (or standardly) regarded.[19]

Levinson is aware that such a definition depends on there already being a work of art prior to any work the definition applies to. In 1979, Levinson says that art that he calls "ur-arts" is required to get the defini-

tion going. But how do ur-arts become art? Levinson says it can be stipulated that ur-arts are art and the definition gets the first bite it needs.

Davies discusses and criticizes various aspects of Levinson's definition at considerable length. For example, he expresses doubt whether
Levinson's notion of *correct* or *standard* regard in his definition can be
worked out without some institutional aspects. In connection with this
and other considerations, Davies concludes, "something more than intentions or unstructured cultural practices is needed if we are to explain, on
the one hand, the extraordinary diversity of art-making activities and of
artworks, and, on the other, the continuing unity of the concept of an
artwork."[20]

Another detail of Levinson's definition, namely, the restriction of
"having an appropriate properietary right," seem to me to involve a difficulty. Suppose a starving artist steals canvas, stretchers, brushes, and tubes
of paint from an art supply store and with these materials paints, signs,
and sells a painting. Now clearly the artist has committed a crime in steal-
ing materials, and since the material are stolen, he has no properietary
right to them. But surely our artist has created a work of art from the
stolen materials. The artist may not legally own the painting he has created
and may have committed another crime in selling it, but whoever the
painting belongs to, it is art.

These two criticisms are, however, matters of detail. I want now to focus
on a more global aspect of Levinson's definition. The point I want to
examine is one that Levinson himself raises about his own theory in a
1993 article. In this article, Levinson has second thoughts about his earlier
view that ur-arts can be stipulated to be art. But if ur-arts are not stipulated to be art, then the original definition cannot get started – that is, if
ur-arts are not art, then, according to the definition, there could not be
any subsequent art. There is then a regress of sorts. I shall let Levinson's
own words show how he proposes to deal with the situation:

> In order to stop this regress, it seems that one of two concessions must be
> made. The first would be to finally grant objects of the *ur*-arts the status of
> art, but admit that they are so in a different sense than applies to all else
> subsequent accountable as art, for reasons that are now plain: they are art
> not because modelled on *earlier* art, but rather because *later*, unquestioned,
> art has sprung from them. The second would be to keep objects of the *ur*-
> arts as non-art, but then to acknowledge that products of the *first* arts, those
> following the *ur*-arts, are art in a sense close to but not identical to that
> applying to all else subsequently accountable as art, in that their arthood
> consists in being projected for regard that some preceding *ur*-art object
> (rather than some preceding *art* object) was correctly accorded.

Either way, the theory's claim to have unearthed a sense of "art" applying univocally to everything in the extension of "art" must be slightly tem-
pered. However, since the tempering required is confined to the very earliest
stages of the story of art, the universality of the analysis of arthood offered
is not, I think, seriously compromised."[21]

Levinson's first alternative, which is to grant ur-arts arthood because
later art has sprung from them, has a logical resemblance to his 1979 solution of stipulating ur-arts to be art. In both cases, ur-arts are art but they
acquire arthood in a different way than does all subsequent art. Levinson's
second alternative, which is to say that ur-arts is not art, means that what
he call "first arts" are art because of their relation to non-art (ur-arts),
which means that first arts acquire arthood in a different way than does
all subsequent art.

Levinson is completely aware of the logical nature of his two 1993 solutions to his theory's problem. He is clear that he has not specified a definition that applies to all art. His reaction to his admission that he does
not have a theory of art is very casual; he characterizes his two solutions
as a slight tempering "confined to the very earliest stages of the story of
art." He concludes, "the universality of . . . [his] . . . analysis is not . . . seriously compromised." The universality of his theory is, however, completely
compromised; it is not a theory at all. Levinson's explantion that the slight
"tempering required is confined to the very earliest stages of the story
of art" has the ring of the old joke's punch-line about being 'just a little
pregnant.'

It can be noted that the institutional theory does not have a similar
problem, because it is a structural theory rather than an historical one. For
the institutional theory, the first arts are those that have a place within the
institutional structure that is the artworld when that structure gels – the
gelling may take place over a considerable period of time. Ur-arts are
things that resemble later art but that do not yet have an artworld to
fit into.

In an article published in 1988, Noël Carroll attacks and rejects the
institutional theory of art and presents his historical/narrational account
for *identifying* artworks as a replacement for the institutional theory and
any other theory of art.[22] In two articles published in 1993[23] and 1994,[24]
the contents of which greatly overlap, Carroll renews his attack on the
institutional theory and again explains his narrational scheme.

Carroll thinks that the attempt to define 'art' has been the central
problem for recent philosophies of art. He also thinks that at least one of

the motives of the definers has been to specify a definition that would enable people to identify artworks, i.e., enable them to determine whether a given object is an artwork. Speaking only for myself, I never conceived of the institutional theory or any other art theory as a means for identifying artworks in this way. Rather, I always thought of theories of art as an explanation of why an artwork *is* art. To use large philosophical words, I have always thought of the institutional theory and all other theories of art as having an ontological function rather than an epistemic one. It seems perfectly reasonable to me that even if one had a completely adequate definition of 'art' that it would still be possible that one might not be able to tell whether a given object is a work of art. For example, if the object's history is unknown, it might be impossible to tell if it is an artwork.

Carroll's complaint about the institutional theory in 1994 is that it does not say anything specific about art but is rather just

a necessary framework of coordinated, communicative practices of a certain level of complexity. . . . But in illuminating certain necessary structural features of such practices, Dickie has not really told us anything about art *qua* art. . . . But . . . [this] . . . is not what disputants in the conversation of analytic philosophy expected in the nature of a definition. [This] . . . is no longer playing the game according to its original rules, and it only confuses matters to pretend that a real definition is still in the offing.[25]

I have never attempted to play according to the original rules. First, following Maurice Mandelbaum, I went beyond the exhibited characteristics of artworks in looking for necessary and sufficient conditions, which violates the definitional rules as conceived of by Weitz and others. Following Mandelbaum and Danto, I sought relational characteristics of art that situate it within human culture because I regard the exhibited characteristics used by traditional theories as hopeless as defining characteristics. Second, I explicitly noted the circularity in both versions of the institutional theory; it is this circularity that marks the definitions of the institutional theory as different from the linear definitions required by the orginal rules of what Carroll calls "a real definition." My view is that the necessary and sufficient conditions specified in the institutional theory cannot be understood independently of the institution of art – an institution that is imbibed from early childhood. I never intended or pretended to give a real definition in Carroll's sense. I take it that such a real definition would specify necessary and sufficient conditions that can be known independently of the defined term 'art.' Following Mandelbaum and

Danto, I sought relational characteristics of art that situate it within human culture because I regard the exhibited characteristics used by traditional theories as hopeless as defining characteristics. Carroll misperceives my intent. We are not really disagreeing.

In any event, I find no fault with the historical/narrative scheme that Carroll describes for identifying artworks. His account is self-consciously addressed to the controversial works of the avant-garde, but it applies as well to more conventional art. There is of course little reason to feel a need to identify conventional works as artworks, but Carroll's procedure could be applied to them. The interesting cases are the contested avant-garde ones. When faced with an object, the artwork identity of which is contested or uncertain, Carroll proposes that the solution lies in telling a *true* narrative that relates the object to earlier undoubted art objects or events. If such a story "links the contested work to preceding art making practices and contexts in such a way that the work under fire can be seen to be the intelligible outcome of recognizable modes of thinking and making of a sort already commonly adjudged to be artistic," then the object is identified as an artwork.[26]

Carroll's scheme resembles Levinson's in its structure – in both cases present artworks are related to earlier artworks. But whereas this procedure generates a particular problem for Levinson's attempt at definition, Carroll is not faced with this problem because he is not trying to define 'art,' merely to identify artworks.

Carroll raises an important question about his own narrational theory – the question of whether the kind of narrations he has in mind might result in identifying nonartworks as art. The example he mentions is Van Gogh's severed ear. Suppose, he says, that a true narrative could be constructed that relates the ear to an attempt by Van Gogh "to symbolize the plight of his artistic conviction in the face of Gauguin's criticisms."[27] Even if such a true story could be told, Carroll says that would not suffice to identify Van Gogh's ear as an artwork. Carroll then compares Van Gogh's mutilation to a twentieth-century artwork – the self-mutilation of a present-day artist. Why is Van Gogh's mutilation not an artwork when the mutilation of the present-day artist is? The reason Carroll says is that the earlier one lacks a framework that the later one has. Carroll describes this framework as follows:

> in order to establish the art status of a contested work, one needs not only to tell an identifying narrative that connects the work in question with acknowledged art practices, but, as well, one needs to establish that the

thinking and making that the identifying narrative reconstructs be localized to activities that occur within recognizable *artworld systems of presentation* – i.e., artforms, media and genres which are available to the *artist* and *the artworld public* under discussion. That is, identifying narratives must be constrained to track only processes of thinking and making conducted inside the *framework of artworld systems of presentation* or recognizable expansions thereof. Moreover, where this constraint is honored, identifying narratives will not commit the error of overinclusiveness. (italics mine)[28]

It turns out that the framework Carroll describes for constraining identifying narratives is made up of the central notions of the institutional theory of art – a theory that Carroll has rejected as a real definition. Since, however, the institutional theory's definition is not a real definition in his sense, Carroll's use of the institutional theory as the framework within which his narrational scheme for identifying art operates causes no logical problem. In fact, Carroll's account for identifying art is nested within the institutional theory.

Davies, writing in 1991 with only Carroll's 1988 article in view, anticipates Carroll's view as nesting within the institutional theory. Davies writes:

> Unless Carroll's narrational strategies are themselves structured by the Artworld context, appeal to them cannot easily explain the unity of the concept of art in view of the long and varied history of art practices and the many nonart practices repeated, amplified, or repudiated within art practices. . . . It is not clear to me how talk of cultural practices founded on repetition and the like can reveal such principles without themselves presupposing a framework for such practices. To presuppose such a framework is to move in the direction of an institutional account.[29]

II

I now turn to the alternative way of classifying theories of art and/or aspects of such theories that I mentioned at the beginning of this chapter.

Human beings, chimpanzees, lions, tigers, bower birds, bees, spiders, mosquitoes, and the like are biological natural kinds, and, I suppose, some or all of the things that members of such various species do can be called 'natural-kind activities.' Gathering food, stalking prey, eating, mating, building nests, constructing the elaborate courtship bowers that bower birds do, living solitarily, and living in social groups are examples of natural-kind activities. Human beings and some other species exhibit cultural-kind activities: particular ways of living together, particular ways of hunting, particular ways of raising food, rituals of eating, and marriage, for example. Some cultural-kind activities are particular ways that in one way or another human beings have come to organize their natural-kind activities. Such activities are in some sense invented by the members of a particular group and are passed on by learning. Cultural-kind activities sometimes involve a conventional element, since there is sometimes a variety of ways to organize a given activity. An example of a cultural-kind activity that does not involve convention is painting. If one creates a painting, one does so by putting some kind of paint of a surface. This is not to say that painting cannot involve conventions; symbols in paintings involve conventions and depictions may involve conventions. The initiation of a cultural-kind activity will in some way or other have involved planning, although I do not mean to suggest that they are initiated at a stroke by a law-giver as mythology favors. Such planning may have been piecemeal, fragmentary, and have taken place over a period of time and in an interrupted way.

Cultural-kind behavior is not written in the genes in the way that natural-kind behavior is, but it is nevertheless remarkably resistant to change. If the pattern of a cultural-kind activity does alter over time, there will always be conservative resistance to change.

Cultural-kind activities are carried out in a self-conscious way in the sense that those doing the activities are aware or could become aware that the activities are aspects of their group cultural life. It is possible for someone to become aware that another group carries out an activity, say, marriage, in a different way and thus be aware at some level that a particular cultural-kind activity involves a conventional aspect. A reflective person might realize that a particular cultural-kind activity has a conventional element even without knowledge of other groups.

The distinction between natural-kind and cultural-kind activities can be used as a basis for classifying theories of art.

A natural-kind theory of art would be one in which it is claimed that art first emerged as a result of a natural-kind activity and that art has continued to be created as the result of natural-kind behavior. Of course, this kind of theory can accommodate cultural aspects in the art-creating process – for example, the cultural phenomenon of painting in the impressionist style – but it would maintain that the creative process itself is at bottom a natural-kind activity. A theorist, for example, who claims that art is the expression of emotion presents a natural-kind theory of art, for the expression of emotion is a clear example of natural-kind behavior.

Cultural matters are frequently involved when emotion is expressed but the expression of emotion itself is a natural-kind phenomenon with evolutionary roots in animal behavior of the sort exhibited by a dog when it growls at other dogs as it eats. The theories that I designated 'psychological' in chapter 1 are natural-kind theories of art.

Monroe Beardsley defines art as "an intentional arrangement of conditions for affording experiences with marked aesthetic character." If it is assumed that human beings are naturally attracted to basic aesthetic qualities of the kind Beardsley has in mind – unity, brightness, shininess, intense color, and the like – and seek experiences of them, Beardsley also presents a natural-kind theory of art. For both Beardsley and the expression theorists the creation of art is just a spontaneous, natural-kind activity on the same level with eating and mating. So far as the creation of art is concerned, Beardsley and the expression theorist conceive of human beings as being very much like bower birds when they construct their courtship bowers. Of course bower birds no doubt carry on their activity in a purely instinctive way, whereas for Beardsley works of art are made by artists by their "own free originative power."[30] Nevertheless, Beardsley's account involves only natural-kind activities – intentional action for foreseen results and the enjoyment of aesthetic qualities.

If Carroll's view of narrationally identifying an artwork is taken as he originally presented it – as the identifying of a present object as art by showing by means of a true narrative that it is an intelligible outcome of earlier art – then his view is not classifiable by means of the natural/cultural activities distinction. This is so because Carroll's account tells us nothing general about art, only that a particular object can be linked to another particular object. Of course, his view is not supposed to be a philosophy of art or a definition of 'art,' so it is not surprising that it cannot be classified by means of criteria for classifying theories of art.

On the other hand, if Carroll's view is taken as he worked it out in 1993, then it has been transformed into an account for identifying art *within* the institutional theory of art, as I understand the institutional theory. In this case, his theory would be classifiable in the same way that the institutional theory would be classifiable by means of the natural/cultural distinction.

The central notion of Levinson's theory of art is an historical relation that relates an artwork at a particular time to an artwork at an earlier time. This central aspect of the theory does not hint at whether an artwork is created as the result of a natural-kind or a cultural-kind activity. In addition to this central notion there are three other conditions specified by

Levinson. The condition of nonpassingly intending does not commit the theory in either of the two directions; such intentions could be involved with either natural-kind or cultural-kind activities. The condition of having a proprietary right implies a cultural phenomenon, although there is no obvious connection between property rights and the notion of what it is that makes something art. The condition of standard or correct regard suggests, as Davies notes,[31] an institutional and, hence, a cultural matter. The central historical notion of Levinson's theory and the nonpassingly intending condition are noncommital with regard to natural-kind or cultural-kind activities. The proprietary right condition is a cultural matter, but it is in fact irrelevant to arthood. Only the standard or correct regard condition inclines the theory in the direction of cultural-kind activities. But even this last condition is not one that Levinson requires an artist to have any actual knowledge of. He writes:

> I would urge that there can be private, isolated art which is constituted as art in the mind of the artist – and on no ones's behalf but his own and that of *potential* experiencers of it. . . . Consider a solitary Indian along the Amazon, who steals off from his non-artistic tribe to arrange coloured stones in a clearing, not outwardly investing them with special position in the world. Might not this also be art (and, note, before any future curator decides it is)?[32]

Levinson clearly thinks that the arranged colored stones are art even though his imagined Indian has no conception of art in mind in any sense of 'in mind.' On Levinson's view, the cultural condition of standardly or correctly regarding the stones can be fulfilled without the person or persons who so regard them having any notion that such a regard is a cultural phenomenon for persons in another culture. Thus, the one condition of Levinson's theory that connects it to cultural-kind activity is such a weak one that, according to the theory, art can be made by someone without any knowledge of the content of the condition. In the end, it is perhaps best to classify Levinson's theory as a natural-kind theory of art. Levinson's imagined Indian's art depends on the Indian's natural-kind activity of admiring the aesthetic qualities of the colored stones.

Danto's 1964 account in "The Artworld" by contrast with the above theories is clearly a cultural-kind theory of art because it claims, in some not very clear way, that it is art theories that make art possible. The formulation and holding of art *theories*, even natural-kind theories of art, are surely cultural-kind affairs, and, thus, if an art theory is what makes art possible, then Danto's account is a cultural-kind theory of art. Later, as noted, Danto began claiming that being about something is a necessary condition of art, and his 1981 book amplified the aboutness thesis into a full-blown theory of art. On Noël Carroll's account of Danto's later theory, to repeat what was said earlier, the theory specifies that a work of art is (1) about something, (2) projects a point-of-view, (3) by means of rhetorical ellipsis, (4) requires interpretation, and (5) the work and interpretation requires an art historical context. The first four items that Carroll discriminates in Danto's later theory fit within the language domain. If, as I take it to be, language is a natural-kind activity, then the first four items of his theory are natural-kind items. The fifth and final item which involves an art historical context, however, is clearly a cultural-kind matter. Danto's later theory, thus, appears to be a mixture of natural-kind and cultural-kind elements, just as earlier when considered for another perspective it was seen to be a mixture of functional and procedural elements. In the case of Danto's later theory, the natural-kind/cultural-kind distinction classifies aspects of his mixed theory.

The institutional theory of art, in either its earlier or its later version, is clearly a cultural-kind theory because it takes a cultural, institutional structure to be the neccessary and sufficient matrix for works of art. Of course, a cultural-kind theory of art will not deny that the content of art can involve natural-kind activities, for example, the enjoyment of the basic aesthetic qualities of the kind Beardsley has in mind, but it would not make such activities defining. For the institutional theory, various natural-kind activities may show up in various artworks, but there is no reason to think that any one natural-kind activity is or needs to be present in every artwork.[33]

The institutional theory of art has frequently been criticized for overlooking the historical dimension of art – the dimension so emphasized by Danto, Levinson, Carroll, and others. The institutional theory, however, is a structural theory rather than an historical one; it does not neglect art history, rather it just does not view it as being involved in the defining of 'art.' All of the talk about art history, as presented by Danto, Carroll and others, is perfectly consistent with the institutional theory, and, as noted in the case of Carroll, can be nested within the institutional theory.

Notes

1   Stephen Davies, *Definitions of Art* (Cornell University Press, 1991), p. 243.
2   Monroe Beardsley, "In Defense of Aesthetic Value," *Proceedings and Addresses of the American Philosophical Association* (Newark, Del.: American Philosophical Association, 1979), p. 729.

3   Dickie, *The Art Circle* (New York: Haven, 1984), pp. 49–68.

4   Davies, *Definitions of Art*, pp. 78–114.

5   Arthur Danto, "The Artworld," reprinted in *Aesthetics: A Critical Anthology* (New York: St. Martin's Press, 1989), ed. G. Dickie, R. Sclafani, and R. Roblin, second edition, p. 180.

6   Arthur Danto, "Artworks and Real Things," *Theoria*, Parts 1–3, pp. 1–17. Reprinted in *Aesthetics: A Critical Anthology* (New York: St. Martin's Press, 1977), first edition, ed. G. Dickie and R. Sclafani, pp. 551–62. All references are to page numbers in this anthology.

7   Arthur Danto, "The Transfiguration of the Commonplace," *The Journal of Aesthetics and Art Criticism* (Winter 1974), pp. 139–48.

8   Arthur Danto, *The Transfiguration of the Commonplace* (Cambridge, Mass.: Harvard University Press, 1981), p. 212.

9   Noël Carroll, "Essence, Expression, and History: Arthur Danto's Philosophy of Art," in *Danto and His Critics*, ed. Mark Rollins (Blackwell, Cambridge, Mass.: 1993), pp. 99–100.

10 Danto, "Artworks and Real Things," p. 561.

11 Danto, "Art and Meaning" in *Theories of Art Today*, ed. N. Carroll (University of Wisconsin Press, 2000), p. 133.

12 Danto, *The Transfiguration of the Commonplace*, p. 78.

13 Davies, *Definitions of Art*, p. 84.

14 Ibid., p. 87.

15 Dickie, *The Art Circle*, pp. 81–4.

16 I wish to thank an anonymous reader of the material in this chaper when it was submitted for publication as an article for the comment that made this last clarification necessary.

17 Ira Newman, Review of *Definitions of Art* in *Canadian Philosophical Reviews*, p. 183.

18 Jerrold Levinson, "Defining Art Historically," *The British Journal of Aesthetics* 19 (1979): 232–50.

19 Ibid., p. 240.

20 Davies, *Definitions of Art*, p. 179.

21 Jerrold Levinson, "Extending Art Historically," *The Journal of Aesthetics and Art Criticism* 51 (1993): 421–2.

22 Noël Carroll, "Art, Practice, and Narrative," *The Monist* 71 (1988): 140–56.

23 Noël Carroll, "Historical Narratives and the Philosophy of Art," *The Journal of Aesthetics and Art Criticism* 51 (1993): 313–26.

24 Noël Carroll, "Identifying Art," in *Institutions of Art* (The Pennsylvania State University Press, 1994), ed. Robert J. Yanal, pp. 3–38.

25 Ibid., pp. 12–13.

26 Noël Carroll, "Historical Narratives and the Philosophy of Art," p. 316.

27 Ibid., p. 324.

28 Ibid.

29 Davies, *Definitions of Art*, p. 169.
30 Monroe Beardsley, "Is Art Essentially Institutional?" in *Culture and Art*, ed. Lars Aagaard-Mogensen (Atlantic Highlands, NJ, 1976), p. 196.
31 Davies, *Definitions of Art*, p. 174.
32 Jerrold Levinson, "Defining Art Historically," p. 233.
33 I wish to thank the same anonymous reader thanked in endnote 16 for the comment that made this last clarification necessary.

4

History of the Institutional Theory of Art

Prologue

In response to a variety of criticisms, I have made four tries over the years to formulate an institutional definition of 'art.' By an institutional account I mean the idea that works of art are art because of the position they occupy within an institutional context. My first try was in 1969 in a journal article.[1] The next two tries – in 1971[2] and 1974[3] – were rather minor attempts at revision. In 1984, I attempted a major overhaul of the theory.[4] I shall call the first three formulations 'the earlier version of the institutional theory.' I shall call the fourth and last formulation 'the later version of the institutional theory.' In the first try (of the earlier version), I specified the definition of 'art' as follows:

> A work of art in the descriptive sense is (1) an artifact (2) upon which society or some sub-group of a society has conferred the status of candidate for appreciation.[5]

I soon realized that speaking of society or some subgroup of society conferring candidacy for appreciation gave the wrong impression that works of art are created by society or a subgroup of society acting as whole, an impression I had not intended. Here and in all subsequent discussions of the institutional theory, I have been trying to capture what goes on when art is created by artists, whether it be a single person painting a picture or a group making a movie. Even in this very first article and despite the perhaps misleading language of the definition, I explicitly stated that the status of candidate for appreciation "must be conferrable by a single person's treating an artifact as a candidate for appreciation. . . ."[6] This quote makes it clear then that even at this early date the theory focuses on the actions of artists when they create art.

In 1971, with a eye to removing this possible wrong impression about who creates art, I reformulated the definition to read:

> A work of art in the classifactory sense is (1) an artifact (2) upon which some person or persons acting on behalf of a certain social institution (the artworld) has conferred the status of candidate for appreciation.[7]

In 1974, I formulated the definition in virtually the same way.

> A work of art in the classificatory sense is (1) an artifact (2) a set of the aspects of which has had conferrred upon it the status of candidate for appreciation by some person or persons acting on behalf of a certain social institution (the artworld).[8]

In both of these slightly later formulations, I spoke of "some person or persons," that is, artist or artists, conferring the status of candidate for appreciation in order to avoid the impression that society acted as a whole to make art.

Despite the conscious care I have employed after the first formulation to avoid the misunderstanding about how art is created according to the institutional theory, a misinterpretation of my view on just this point has become widely accepted. Richard Wollheim in his 1987 book, *Painting As An Art*, focusing only on the earlier version of the theory, attributes to me the view I had taken such pains to avoid. Specifically, Wollheim attributes to me the view that, according to the earlier version of the theory, art is made by representatives of the artworld who meet and jointly act as a group to confer status on certain objects. Wollheim then ridicules this absurd view:

> Does the art-world really nominate representatives? If it does, when, where, and how, do these nominations take place? Do the representatives, if they exist, pass in review all candidates for the status of art, and do they then, while conferring this status on some, deny it to others? What record is kept of these conferrals, and is the status itself subject to revision? If so, at what intervals, how, and by whom? And, last but not least, Is there really such a thing as the art-world, with the coherence of a social group, capable of having representatives, who are in turn capable of carrying out acts that society is bound to endorse?[9]

(Notice that according to Wollheim the institutional theory is about the conferring of the status of *art*, whereas my three earlier definitions speak of the conferring of the status of candidacy for appreciation, but I shall ignore this detail.)[10]

Arthur Danto picked up Wollheim's version of what my earlier view is and incorporated it into a paper on which I was a commentator. I informed Danto that this was a gross misinterpretation my earlier view, but when his paper was published, he still attributed this view to me. Subsequently, Danto attributed this same view to me in one of his columns in *The Nation*.[11] I wrote a letter of protest to the editor which was published along with Danto's reply to my letter. In his reply, Danto calls Wollheim's account the *core* of the institutional theory and says, "Nor can there be great doubt that this core plays a central role though George Dickie's various formulations of the I[nstitutional] T[heory of] A[rt]. . . ." Danto then asserts that Dickie "has lately come to specify that 'some person or persons' must be an artist (or some artists), but in my [Danto's] view this is a step backwards from the robust form in which the [institutional theory of art] is best understood."[12] Danto is saying that the version of the institutional theory that Wollheim ridicules is the best way to understand the earlier version of the theory.

First, the so-called core had never been my understanding of the earlier version. Second, it is not *lately* that I have specified artists to be the creators of art. I put "person or persons" into the definition in 1971 for this purpose. And when I made this change so long ago I also wrote:

> A number of persons are required to make up the social institution of the artworld, but only one person is required to act on behalf of or as agent of the artworld and confer the status of candidate for appreciation. Many works of art are never seen by anyone but the persons who create them, but they are still works of art. The status in question may be acquired by *a single person's treating an artifact as a candidate for appreciation*. Of course nothing prevents a group of persons conferring the status, but it is usually conferred by a single person, the artist who creates the artifact.[13]

When I spoke of a group conferring the status of candidate for appreciation, I had in mind, not the whole artworld or a group of its nominated representatives, but a group that makes a movie, puts on a play, or the like. Furthermore, in the original article of 1969, although I did not give many examples of art-making, I did speak of Duchamps's artistic act of creating "Fountain." I wrote, "Duchamp's act took place within a certain institu-

tional setting . . .", but I did not say that some group of artworld representatives had to also act or concur in Duchamp's act.[14]

By the way, Wollheim was not the first one to attribute what Danto
calls the "robust" version of the institutional theory of art to me, but he
was, I think, the first to attribute it and to criticize it. As for this "robust"
form of the theory, I believe that it is best embraced by aestheticians of
the species *Paranthropus robustus*.[15] Unfortunately, the "robust" view has
now even been attributed to me in the recently published *Cambridge
Dictionary of Philosophy*.[16]

An article by Monroe Beardsley convinced me that there was a kind
of inconsistency between each of the first three definitions and the texts
with which I had surrounded them.[17] In the texts, I had spoken of the
institution of art as an informal institution, but in the definitions which
purport to encapsulate and describe the institution, I used the very formal
language "conferred upon" and "acting on behalf."

Consequently, in *The Art Circle*[18] (the 1984 formulation and the later
version of the theory), I dropped the formal language. Also, in this fourth
attempt, I specified five definitions – definitions of what I regard as the
core notions of the institutional theory of art.

An artist is a person who participates with understanding in the making
of a work of art.

A work of art is an artifact of a kind created to be presented to an artworld public.

A public is a set of persons the members of which are prepared in some
degree to understand an object which is presented to them.

The artworld is the totality of all artworld systems.

An artworld system is a framework for the presentation of a work of
art by an artist to an artworld public.[19]

There is absolutely no element in any of these five definitions that gives
the slightest impression that anything other than artists, as everyone ordinarily understands artists, create art. The fact that I specify a definition of
'artist' as one of the five definitions makes it clear how I understand art to
be created. Both Wollheim and Danto published their comments well after
the appearance of the later version (Wollheim even refers to the later
version). It is unfortunate that Wollheim did not take sufficient notice of
the later version or that Danto did not take any notice of the later version

because either would have provided a better basis for a more accurate interpretation of the earlier version. In the later version, at the beginning of *The Art Circle*, I discussed at considerable length the misinterpretation of my earlier view that had already been made by some, which is exactly the same misinterpretation that Wollheim and Danto made later.[20]

Notice also that in the later version that reference to candidacy for appreciation is also dropped. Candidacy for appreciation had originally been included in order to distinguish between those aspects of a work of art to which appreciation and/or criticism ought to be directed – for example, the representation and spatial organization visible on the surface of a painting – and those aspects of an artwork to which appreciation and/or criticism ought not to be directed, for example, the color of the back of a painting. This distinction is still important, but I decided that it was not one that needed to be addressed within the institutional theory of art.

At this point I want to take note of an argument invented and used by Danto that I have adopted. Danto envisions visually indistinguishable pairs of objects: "Fountain" and a urinal that looks just like it, the painting "The Polish Rider" and an accidently produced paint and canvas object that looks just like it, Warhol's "Brillo Box" and a real brillo box that looks just like it. Danto notes that the first member of each of the pairs is a work of art while the second member is not. He concludes that there is a context that the eye cannot descry that accounts for the first member's being a work of art and the second not. That is, the first member of each pair is embedded in a context that the second member of each pair is not. Danto then gives his account of what this context is. I accept Danto's argument but I give a different account of what the context is, namely, the institutional account embodied in the definitions I have given. The visually-indistinguishable-objects argument of course applies, with suitable adjustments, to artworks outside the domain of visual art.

The Two Versions of the Institutional Theory

In all formulations of the theory, I have tried to formulate what I first called a 'descriptive' and subsequently called a 'classifactory' sense of 'work of art.' That is, I have always sought to define a value-neutral sense of art. I believe this is necessary because we sometimes speak of bad art and worthless art. If works of art are defined as necessarily valuable, it would make it difficult or impossible to speak of bad or worthless art. Thus, I believe that the basic theory of art is about a value-neutral sense of art. Notice that this basic theory is about the members of the class of works of art: some members are excellent, some members are mediocre, and some members are bad. The general *activity* of creating artworks is of course a valuable activity, but it is the members of the class of works of art that the institutional theory is focused on. By the way, not all the products of a valuable activity need to be valuable, although a certain percentage of them would have to be. Furthermore, I do not deny that the expression 'work of art' can be used in an evaluative way. Thus, there is an evaluative sense of 'work of art.' My definition of 'work of art,' however, is supposed to capture a basic, nonevaluative sense of the expression, which of course includes all the works of art to which the evaluative sense applies as well as all the mediocre and bad works.

Both the earlier and the later versions of the theory are responses to the view that 'art' is an open concept that cannot be defined in terms of necessary and sufficient conditions.[21] The general claim of the institutional theory is that if we stop looking for *exhibited* (easily-noticed) characteristics of artworks such as representationality, emotional expressivity, and the others that the traditional theorists focused on, and instead look for characteristics that artworks have as a result of their relation to their cultural context, then we can find defining properties.[22] The theories of art formulated by the traditional theorists are easily refuted by counterexample because the immense diversity of artworks furnishes many examples of works of art that lack the properties specified as defining by the traditional theories. On the other hand, no artwork, no matter how unusual, can escape its relations to its cultural context. The problem is to find the defining relational properties of artworks to their culture and to characterize them correctly.

One problem of my three earlier attempts at definition already noted is the formal language used in the formulations of the definitions; the changes in the definitions of the later version are aimed at arriving at an overall account that is consistently informal. Another problem of the earlier account is that it claimed that the artifactuality of artworks could be achieved in two ways: (1) by being crafted in one traditional way or another, or (2) by being conferred. The conferring of artifactuality in the earlier version was supposed to account for the artistic artifactuality of found art, Dadaist art, and the like, cases in which no traditional crafting occurs. I subsequently came to believe that artifactuality is not something that can be conferred, but is a characteristic that must be achieved in some way. In the later version, I tried to show that found art, Dadaist art, and the like possess a minimal artistic artifactuality as the result of artists *using* found objects, manufactured objects (Dada), and such as media within the artworld. Thus, for example, Duchamp *used* a plumbing artifact (a urinal) to produce the scupture-like artwork "Fountain." "Fountain" is a manufactured artifact as the result of what happened in a factory *and* an artistic artifact as the result of what Duchamp did with a factory-manufactured object – it is a double artifact. Of course, ordinary paintings are double artifacts too, since artists construct them using manufactured items: paints, canvas, and the like. *Fountain* is like what anthropologists have in mind when they speak of unaltered stones found in conjunction with human or human-like fossils as artifacts. The used object is a complex thing made up of a simpler thing and its use – the urinal and its use, a rock and its use, and so on.

The Later Version of the Institutional Theory

I now move to the remainder of the content of the later version of institutional theory, and I shall do so by commenting on the five definitions in the order that I listed them above.

An artist is a person who participates with understanding in the making of a work of art.

The notion of *understanding* is very important here. There are two things to be understood. First, there is the general idea of art that must be understood so that an individual knows what kind of activity he or she is involved in. Being an artist is a mode of behavior that is learned in one way or another from one's culture. Second, there is the understanding of the particular artistic medium or media that an individual is using. Such understanding need not involve great mastery of a medium for even beginners can create art. On the other hand, a person can have understanding of both of the above things, participate in the making of a work of art, and still not participate as an artist. Stage carpenters and primers of canvases participate in a way in the making of artworks and in almost all cases no doubt have the requisite understandings, but they do not participate in the artist *role* because what they do can be done without the requisite understandings. A primer of canvases has a very different role from that of an assistant who helps a master with a painting.

The definition of 'artist' depends on the notion of work of art and naturally leads on to a definition of 'work of art.'

A work of art is an artifact of a kind created to be presented to an artworld public.

In the first three formulations of the definition of 'work of art,' I broke it into two parts. The first part involved artifactuality and the second part involved the conferring of candidacy for appreciation. Both conferring and candidacy for appreciation have been dropped, and the definition is not broken up in any way. In the later version, the defining of 'work of art' is approached entirely through the *creating* of an artifact. Focusing on artifactuality in this way is a return to tradition, for from ancient times on philosophers of art have been concerned to theorize about the class of objects that is generated by a particular kind of human making. Philosophers have been interested in these objects precisely because they are human artifacts. According to the later definition, the *status* of art is achieved through the creating of a certain sort of artifact. Such an artifact is one that is intended to be a particular sort of thing, namely, the kind of thing created to be presented to an artworld public. Notice that putting it in this way leaves open the possibility that artworks can be created that are *never* presented to anyone, for the definition requires only that an artwork be a kind of thing to be presented. I have phrased the definition in this way to allow for the untold artworks that have been created but which for one reason or another have not reached any artworld public. By the way, in using the word 'kind' here, I am using it in a very general way and am not using it to suggest kinds or genres within art such as novels, painting, or the like.

I should note that such things as playbills, exhibition catalogues, and the like are created to be presented to artworld publics but they are not artworks. They, however, are derived from artworks, and the definition is intended to apply to *primary* objects of the artworld domain.

The definition of 'work of art' makes essential use of the notions of *public* and *artworld*, so these two notions need definition and discussion.

A public is a set of persons the members of which are prepared in some degree to understand an object which is presented to them.

'Public' as here defined is not tied solely to the artworld − it is a notion of general application. There is a voting public, a basketball public, a dog-show public, and the like, as well as a painting public, a stage public, and other artworld publics. A public as such is just a set of persons with knowledge of how to understand and deal with a particular kind of situation. A member of an artworld public has characteristics that parallel those of an artist: (1) a general idea of art and (2) a minimal understanding of the medium or media of a particular art form.

Does an artist always have in mind a public for his or her work? Suppose an artist deliberately withholds a work from actual presentation? If an artist does so because he or she judges it unworthy, then it is being judged as unworthy for a public and is thus being counted as a kind of thing created to be presented to a public. Suppose an artist withholds a work because he or she regards it as too revealing in some way. In this kind of case, an artist has a public in mind because it is a public to whom the work would be revealing. In cases when a work is deliberately withheld from a public, there is a *double intention*, that is, there is an intention to create a thing of a kind to be presented to an artworld public, but there is also an intention not to actually present it.

Now for the definition and discussion of the other notion used in defining 'work of art,' namely 'artworld.'

The artworld is the totality of artworld systems.

This means that the artworld is a collection of different systems – painting, literature, theater, and the like. The collection is not a tidy one but is rather one that has been drawn together over time in a somewhat arbitrary way. Why does it include literature, theater, and ballet but not dog shows, horse shows, and circuses? The answer is that the artworld is a cultural construction – something that members of society have collectively made into what it is over time. Although perhaps no one has ever consciously decided that dog shows are excluded from the cultural construction that is the artworld, it has turned out that way. If the history of culture had been a little different, the artworld might also be different and include dog shows. There is a strong chance of there being an element of arbitrariness in every cultural construction simply because they come about as a result of people's behavior over time.

Traditional theories of art try to avoid the untidiness exhibited here by attempting to bind all the diverse works of art together as instances of some characteristic or characteristics of human nature such as the expression of emotion; the characteristic (or characteristics) is used as the essence (or essences) of art. The sheer diversity of artworks, however, destroys the traditional approach. The institutional approach embraces the great diversity and admits to the kind of logical untidiness discussed above. Traditional theories try to discover the essence of art in some aspect of human nature such as the expression of emotion. The institutional theory focuses on human culture and its history.

The definition of 'the artworld' depends entirely on the notion of *artworld system*, which I have defined as follows:

An artworld system is a framework for the presentation of a work of art by an artist to an artworld public.

The first four definitions of the later version have been produced by means of a linear descent, that is, 'artist' is defined in terms of the notion of *work of art*. 'Work of art' is defined in terms of the notions of *public* and *artworld*. 'Public' is defined generally and thus stands outside the linear descent. 'The artworld' continues the linear descent and is defined in terms of the notion of *artworld system*. The definition of 'artworld system,' however, instead of extending the linear descent using more foundational notions, reaches back and uses all four of the earlier defined notions in its definition. Thus, what begins as a linear descent ends up being a circle – the five definitions constitute a circular set. Circularity is a characteristic that traditional theories do not have. For example, expressionism defines 'art' in terms of the expression of emotion, but the definition of the 'expression of emotion' would not involve the notion of art.

Circularity is generally regarded as a logical fault because it is claimed that it fails to give an informative definition or description. For example, when Clive Bell said that significant form is what causes aesthetic emotion and then said that aesthetic emotion is what is caused by significant form, many concluded that they had really not been told anything, and perhaps they had not. Artist, work of art, public, artworld and artworld system, unlike significant form and aesthetic emotion, are not technical notions generated within a theory and in need of a theoretical explanation. The five central notions of the institutional theory are all notions that we all learn at a tender age, and we learn them together as a set. Art teachers and parents teach children how to be artists and how to display their work. Children are taught how to draw and color and how to put their drawing on the refrigerator door for others to see.

What children are being taught are basic *cultural roles* of which every competent member of our society has at least a rudimentary understanding. These cultural roles are, I believe, invented very early on in primitive societies and persist through time into all structured societies. So, when we hear 'artist' and 'work of art' we are not baffled in the way that we are when we hear 'significant form' and 'aesthetic emotion.' When an adult hears 'artist' and 'work of art,' they hear words that they have known the meaning of for a very long time. The circularity of the central notions of the institutional theory thus poses no problem of the understanding of these notions. The fact that the five central notions of the institutional theory are learned together as a set means that they are what I call 'inflected concepts,' a set of concepts that bend in on themselves, presupposing and supporting one another.

There is nothing mysterious about such sets of concepts. I suspect that many of our cultural phenomena involve inflected notions, notions that are interdefined and are learned as a set. The political notions of executive, legistature, judiciary, and law are such a set of concepts.

I noted earlier that artist and artworld public roles come into existence in the most primitive of societies and persist into the most advanced of societies. In their earliest manifestations, the central roles of artist and artworld public pretty much are the culture's artworld. Later, the artworld contains many other roles: art galleries entrepreneurs, museum curators, art critics, art theorists, philosophers of art, and others. All of these sophisticated roles are parasitical on the central roles of artist and artworld public, the cultural framework that persists through time and constitutes the core of the art-making enterprise.

When, someone might ask, did the first work of art come into existence according the institutional theory? First, the institutional theory is a *structural* theory, by which is meant that the theory is about the five defined elements that make up the structure of the art-making enterprise. Thus, according to the institutional theory, the first work of art would be the one that occupied the work of art node of the artworld structure when that structure first gelled. It would of course be very difficult to date the time of such a gelling, although no doubt it has occurred many different times in many different cultures.

Finally, it should be noted that the institutional theory of art is not an attempt to say everything that there is to be said about art. Art does many, many different things that are not touched on by the institutional theory or any other theory of art. Any theory of art, including the institutional theory, attempts to specify defining characteristics, which are going to be rather narrowly restricted and simply will not reflect the broad scope of the things that works of art do.

Richard Wollheim in 1980[23] set out an argument against the institutional theory of art as it was presented in my *Art and the Aesthetic* in 1974.[24] This argument is cited and referred to frequently and many apparently regard it as a definitive refutation of the institutional theory – a sort of killer argument on the model of the Monty Python killer joke. I think it is important to consider and refute this argument in spite of the fact that I no longer hold the 1974 version of the institutional theory. I think Wollheim's argument is completely spurious, and further I think it is important to clarify the issue in case anyone thinks his argument applies to the later version of the institutional theory.[25]

Wollheim begins the article in which the argument at issue occurs by denying that there are evaluative and other senses of 'work of art,' – senses that I had tried to distinguish. He claims that what I called senses of the term are cases of ellipsis and metaphor. He writes that what my examples "show is that 'art' is often used idiomatically or in ways which cannot be understood simply on the basis of knowing its *primary* meaning" (italics mine).[26] Whether there are different senses or simply cases of ellipsis and metaphor here is not important, as Wollheim's remark about *primary* meaning shows; the institutional theory has always been an attempt to deal with what Wollheim calls the *primary* meaning of 'work of art.' Whether there are evaluative or other senses of 'work of art' or whether there are only ellipses and metaphors, it is the primary meaning of 'work of art' that is at issue. (Whether a given usage of a word is metaphorical or has a new sense depends, I suppose, on whether or not a metaphor has recently died.)

I turn now to Wollheim's argument. His argument takes the form of a dilemma. He writes:

> Is it to be presumed that those who confer status upon some artifact do so for good reasons, or is there no such presumption? Might they have no reason, or bad reasons, and yet their action be efficacious given that they themselves have the right status – that is, they represent the artworld?[27]

If, Wollheim claims, the institutionalist takes the first horn of the dilemma, his theory is not *institutional*, but if he takes the second horn it is not a theory of *art*.[28] Taking the first horn, Wollheim argues, would make the theory noninstitutional because it would be the possession of the characteristic referred to by the good reason that makes the artifact a work of art. As far as I can tell Wollheim never says or indicates why taking the second horn would prevent the theory from being a theory of art.

As noted earlier, Wollheim caricatures the institutional theory as holding that there are artworld representatives who are nominated and have meetings to confer the status of art. In *Art and the Aesthetic*, I did speak of a person (an artist) acting on behalf of the artworld to confer the status of candidate for appreciation because of his or her imagination and because of his or her knowledge of the artworld. I did not say that the status of candidate for appreciation is conferred because of a *status* that a person has. Perhaps the dilemma could be rewritten as:

> Is it to be presumed that those who confer status upon some artifact do so for good reasons, or is there no such presumption? Might they have no reason, or bad reasons, and yet their action be efficacious given that they themselves have the *requisite knowledge and imagination*.

Having stated the alleged dilemma, Wollheim begins a discussion of the first horn:

> If the representatives of the artworld, setting out to confer status upon an artifact, are effective only if they have certain reasons which justify their selection of this rather than that artifact, does it not look as though what it is for an artifact to be a work of art is for it to satisfy these reasons? But, if this is so, then what the representatives of the artworld do is inappropriately called 'conferment' of status: what they do is to 'confirm' or 'recognize' status in that the artifact enjoys the status prior to their action: and the consequence is that reference to their action ought to drop out of the definition of art as at best inessential.[29]

In this passage, Wollheim writes as if the institutional theory conceives of *all* art-making as proceeding in the way that Duchamp made his ready-mades – by the "selection of this rather than that artifact." This is misleading. The institutional theory conceives of the great bulk of art-making as proceeding in the traditional ways of painting, sculpting, and so on; it just pictures these procedures as taking place *within a certain institutional framework*. In any event, Wollheim queries in an assertive manner, "does it not look as though what it is for an artifact to be a work of art is for it to satisfy these reasons?" For him, to have a *good* reason means to note that an artifact has a *certain* characteristic, and having that characteristic is what is solely responsible for the artifact's being a work of art. But then after the just quoted passage, he raises the possibility that (1) having a good reason for conferring the status, and (2) the conferring of status are *both* necessary for making art. Wollheim, however, then immediately rejects this possibility and concludes,

> Of course, in the absence of any account of what these reasons are or are likely to be the issue cannot be settled, but it is hard to see how there could be reasons putatively for making an artifact a work of art which were not better thought of as reasons for its being one.[30]

Since Wollheim raises the issue of good reasons, it is puzzling that he does not give at least a brief account of 'what these reasons are or are likely to be.' He does not give even one example of what he has in mind but just keeps referring indeterminately to good reasons. In any event, Wollheim's conclusion is clearly that it is the characteristic referred to by a good reason alone that makes something a work of art and that, therefore, no kind of institutional action is involved in art-making.

In order for this sub-argument concerning the first horn of the dilemma to be persuasive, the last sentence quoted would have to be backed up with further argument or be obviously clinching, which it is not. Wollheim, however, drops this point and changes the subject. First, with regard to his quoted comment concerning reasons, the discussion should be about making an artifact a candidate for appreciation, not about making one a work of art. My actual view in 1974 was that there are two necessary conditions that are jointly sufficient for making a work of art: (1) the producing of an artifact, and (2) the conferring of the candidacy for appreciation. Wollheim is aware of the distinction that I made between being a candidate for appreciation and being a work of art because he specifically alludes to it, saying that for institutionalists "The status conferred is, more specifically, that of being a candidate for appreciation."[31] When setting out his arguments, however, he ignores my actually stated views and writes as if the 1974 version of the institutional theory involves the conferring of the status of work of art. I have in the following tried to deal with this misrepresentation by using the disjunction 'candidate of appreciation or work of art.' Second, his quoted comment concerning reasons is clearly wrong; there could be all sorts of reasons for making an artifact a work of art or for conferring candidacy for appreciation on it that would not be reasons for the artifact's being a work of art or a candidate for appreciation. For example, an artist might have as a good reason for creating a particular work of art or candidate for appreciation that it is intended to promote a particular moral point of view. Let it be assumed that the work of art or candidate for appreciation when created does promote the particular moral point of view. While this is a perfectly good reason for crafting a work of art or candidate for appreciation, intending it to promote a particular moral point of view or actually promoting a particular moral point of view is not something that is responsible for its *being* a work of art or a candidate for appreciation in, for example, the way *crafting* is responsible for its being a work of art or a candidate for appreciation. (I am not assuming that crafting alone is responsible for something's being a work of art or a candidate for appreciation. I do not think that it is.) Crafting a work of art or a candidate for appreciation to realize certain aesthetic qualities would be another typical good reason for such creation, but neither intending the created object to realize these aesthetic qualities nor actually realizing the aesthetic qualities is what is responsible for its being a work of art or candidate for appreciation in, for example, the way crafting is. (Again, I am not saying that crafting alone is the whole story.) Works of *non*art can self-consciously be made by their creators intending these two good reasons and realizing them without either the reasons in mind or the corresponding characteristics in the artifact making or even tending to make their creations into works of art or artworld candidates for appreciation. For example, a religious person might write a tract with the intention to promote a particular moral point of view and realize this end or a tool designer might create a wrench to have certain aesthetic qualities and realize this end. In neither of these two cases would the good reasons in the makers' minds or the corresponding characteristics in the artifacts make or tend to make the created objects into works of art or artworld candidates for appreciation. Wollheim's sub-argument about the first horn of the dilemma just stops in mid-air, drawing an invalid conclusion without any argument. (I remind the reader that in speaking of conferring candidacy for appreciation here I am, for purposes of argument, stepping back into a theory that I no longer hold.)

There are some other good reasons that are worth considering briefly. These are reasons that have figured in various theories of art: the desire to produce a representation, the desire to express an emotion, and so on. These reasons and their corresponding characteristics in artifacts fail as art-making for the same reason that the earlier reasons and corresponding characteristics do, because the desires and these corresponding character-istics can be satisfied and realized by the production of nonart.

After concluding his argument about the first horn of the dilemma, Wollheim challenges the institutionalist to give "some independent evidence . . . for what the representatives of the artworld allegedly do" and to "point to positive practices, conventions, or rules, which are all explicit in the . . . artworld."[32] He writes of the evidence of the kind of artworld actions that he thinks the institutionalist might have in mind:

This need not be evidence for some altogether new action on their part. It could be evidence that a new description is true of some already identified action: that commissioning a piece of music, buying a painting for a gallery, writing a monograph on a sculpture should be redescribed as acts conferring the status of art upon certain artifacts.[33]

This last quotation shows how badly Wollheim has misunderstood what I said in *Art and the Aesthetic*. I was trying to give an account of what goes on when art is created *by artists*. He seems to think I might have been talking about activities such as commissioning music and buying paintings as art-making – activities that revolve around artists and art-making at some considerable distance.

Near the end of his article Wollheim returns to a discussion of the first horn of the dilemma. He says there is a sub-argument that forces an institutionalist to take the first horn of the dilemma, so that the institutionalist "has to say that the conferment of the status of work of art [read candidate for appreciation] upon an artifact depends upon good reasons, with the consequence that conferment ceases to be an essential feature of art and so drops out of the definition of art."[34] Before examining the sub-argument that the institutionalist must accept the good-reasons alternative, consider whether Wollheim's supposed consequence really follows. He says that if good reasons are necessary for conferring the status of arthood or candidacy for appreciation, then conferring drops out as a necessary condition of art or candidacy for appreciation. Consider a parallel case. Presumably having a good reason is required for a king or queen to confer a knighthood. Say that a man has had knighthood conferred on him because he is believed to have slain a dragon. Believing the man to be a dragon-slayer is the good reason that he has had knighthood conferred on him, but he would not be a knight if a king or queen had not conferred the status on him. The conferring does not 'drop out' as a necessary part of becoming a knight because it is done for a good reason. That conferring 'drops out' if a good reason is necessary is just false as a generalization. I do not claim that Wollheim holds such a generalization, but I do not see any reason to think that having a good reason for conferring candidacy for appreciation (or art status) would cause conferring to 'drop out' as necessary in the case of art-making, if, as I thought it was in 1974, conferring were involved in art-making.

Now back to the sub-argument that supposedly forces the institution-alist to accept the good-reasons alternative. Wollheim's argument is that in presenting something as a candidate for appreciation, the presenter must have in mind something about the presented thing that he wants to be appreciated and what he has in mind is what Wollheim is calling a "good reason."[35] It is certainly true that in the creation of art over almost all of its history artists have had good reasons in Wollheim's sense. There are many, many things that artists have wanted appreciated about their art – its aesthetic qualities, its political statement, its moral vision, its stylish verve, and so on and on. But after the practice of art-making, with good reasons invariably present, had been in place for a long time, it occurred to Duchamp and his ilk that they could present candidates for apprecia-tion within the framework of the artworld that they did not expect anyone to appreciate – that is, they presented them in defiance of the usual good reasons. What Duchamp's readymades show is that candidacy for appreciation can be conferred and art created without the usual good reasons. There is perhaps a further analogy between art-making and knight-making. In the days when monarchs had absolute power there were no doubt cases in which the monarch conferred knighthood on persons without having a good reason, while, of course, pretending to have one. The real (bad) reason might be that the person was an old, boyhood friend or the like. Despite the lack of a good reason, such persons would still be knights. I do not wish to suggest that Duchamp had absolute power in the artworld as a monarch had in the political world, but he certainly had the power to be noticed.

But let it be assumed for the sake of argument that readymades are not art and that artists always have had and always will have a good reason for conferring candidacy for appreciation and for making art. What is the significance of having a good reason? Earlier, Wollheim seemed to be claiming that it is the good reason that makes something a candidate for appreciation or art. This was shown to be invalid because nonart can be created with all the same good reasons. What then would be the significance of the fact, if it were a fact, that artists always have a good reason for conferring candidacy for appreciation or making art? None, I think, other than the fact that people typically like to have a good reason for what they do, and in a highly regularized activity such as art-making, it should not be surprising if there were always a good reason for carrying on the activity. I suppose it was this feature of art-making that made the shenanigans of Duchamp and company so upsetting to so many.

Wollheim's sub-argument concerning the first horn of the dilemma fails at every juncture. There are all sorts of reasons for making an artifact a work of art or a candidate for appreciation that are not reasons for its being a work of art or a candidate for appreciation. Moreover, having a good reason for conferring arthood or candidacy for appreciation such as intending to realize certain aesthetic qualities, promote a moral point of view, and the like is *not* what makes an artwork art or something a candidate for appreciation. Also, there is no justification for thinking that having a good reason would cause conferring to 'drop out' as essential, if conferring were involved in art-making.

I turn now to the second horn of Wollheim's dilemma. He quite correctly thinks that an institutionalist will not willingly choose the first horn and will prefer the second. He writes that an institutionalist will deny

> that the representatives of the artworld need to have good reasons for conferring the appropiate status upon an artifact. All that is required (he [the institutionalist] will say) is that they themselves have the appropiate status: to require more is to betray a serious confusion. The confusion would be between the conditions under which something is (or becomes) a work of art and the conditions under which a work of art is a good work of art. To assert that something is a work of art depends, directly or indirectly, only upon status: by contrast, to assert that a work of art is a good work of art does require to be backed up by reasons, and it receives no support from status.[36]

Now as earlier, Wollheim in the passage quoted does not have the second horn stated correctly, but in 1980 I certainly would have chosen the second horn if it asserted that something's being a candidate for appreciation depends on its being conferred by someone with the relevant imagination and knowledge, i.e., someone filling the role of artist. Even if it were the case that there is always a good reason when candidacy for appreciation is conferred, I would choose the second horn in the sense that I would claim that it is not the good reason but the conferring's taking place within the relevant institutional setting that is responsible for the candidate for appreciation becoming an artworld candidate. So, Wollheim has put the wrong words into my mouth. My choice was *not* driven by an attempt to avoid a confusion between being art and being good art; my choice was driven by the desire to describe the process by which art is created, which I then thought involved (in part) the conferring of the candidacy for appreciation . Once it has been shown that, even if there is always a good reason, the institutionalist is not forced to say that it is having a good reason that makes something a candidate for appreci-ation or an artwork, then the second alternative, as I have rewritten it, is not a horn of a dilemma but a perfectly acceptable alternative. Candidacy for appreciation can be conferred and art made independently of having a good reason, even if there is always a good reason. I can accept both horns of Wollheim's dilemma as I have reformulated it. I came to believe that the 1974 account of the institutional theory was wrong but not for the reasons that Wollheim gives.

Wollheim is right on one point, I did then and do now want to avoid confusing being art and being good art. Wollheim apparently thinks it is a mistake to try to distinguish between being art and being good art; he says that making this distinction violates two powerful intuitions that we have. The first intuition appears to be embodied in his assertion, "it seems a well-entrenched thought that reflection upon the nature of art has an important part to play in determining the standards by which works of art are evaluated."[37] If the imitation, the expression, or some such theory of the nature of art were true, then Wollheim's claim would be justified. For example, if the nature of art were imitation, then reflection would no doubt reveal that the better the imitation the better the art. The intuition Wollheim is appealing to here is a theory-laden one. Everything, thus, depends upon the *nature* that is to be reflected on when the nature of art is reflected on. Wollheim's first 'intuition' simply assumes that some par-ticular theory of art other than the institutional theory is true and thereby begs the question. The second intuition "is that there is something impor-tant to the status of being a work of art . . . [and] if works of art derive their status from conferment, and the status may be conferred for no good reason, the importance of the status is placed in serious doubt."[38] The status of being a work of art is important, and the reason is that the class of works of art contains a large number of very valuable items. The class of works of art also contains many works that are mediocre, and many that are bad, and this is the reason that I wish to distinguish between being art and being good art. It is necessary that we have a way to talk about mediocre and bad art.

At the end of his essay, Wollheim comments that the institutionalists have made too much of Duchamp. He writes that institutionalists

have been deeply impressed by the phenomenon of Marcel Duchamp and his readymades. . . . It certainly would be a total misunderstanding of Duchamp's intentions . . . to think that the existence of readymades requires *aesthetic* theory to be *reformulated* in such a way as to represent an object like *Fontaine* as a *central* case of a work of art. On the contrary, it seems more like an extra condition of adequacy upon a contemporary *aesthetic* theory that objects like Duchamp's readymades, which are heavily *ambigious*, highly *provocative*, and altogether *ironical* in their relationship to art, should have this overall characteristic preserved within the theory, or that the theory should be sufficiently sophisticated to recognize such *special cases* as what they are. (italics mine)[39]

A number of comments are in order here. First, the institutional theory is not an aesthetic theory, it is a theory of *art*. Second, the theory does not claim that readymades are *central* cases of works of art; it regards them as works of art that are useful in revealing the matrix in which works of art exist because readymades lack the usual interesting features of art. In Wollheim's terms, the institutional theory regards readymades as works of art that exist independently of the usual good reasons. I have even suggested the possibility that they are not works of art but are revealing in the relevant way because some people mistakenly believed them to be art.[40] (Of course, this last point was made four years after Wollheim's piece was published.) Finally, I have always been aware that readymades are ambigious, provocative, ironical, and are special cases. I doubt that anyone thinks that there cannot be ambigious, provocative and ironical art or art that is a special case in some way.

In closing this chapter on the history of the institutional theory, I note that several philosophers in recent years have developed a theory of art that is institutional or has an institutional aspect. Terry Diffey, in 1969, in an article entitled "The Republic of Art," set forth a kind of institutional theory, but it was not an anthropological sort as mine is.[41] As noted in chapter 2, Stephen Davies, in the process of criticizing my view, sketches an institutional theory of art the central notion of which is that art-making derives from an exercise of authority. He, however, neither develops nor argues for this view. Noël Carroll's account of identifying works of art turns out to presuppose an institutional theory of art when its presuppositions are unpacked.

Notes

1 George Dickie, "Defining Art," *American Philosophical Quarterly*, 1969, pp. 253–6.
2 George Dickie, *Aesthetics: An Introduction* (Indianapolis: Pegasus, 1971), pp. 98–108.

3   George Dickie, *Art and the Aesthetic* (Ithaca, NY: Cornell University Press, 1974), pp. 204.

4   George Dickie, *The Art Circle* (New York: Haven, 1984), p. 116.

5   Dickie, "Defining Art," p. 252.

6   Ibid., p. 252.

7   Dickie, *Aesthetics: An Introduction*, p. 101.

8   Dickie, *Art and the Aesthetic*, p. 34.

9   Richard Wollheim, *Painting As An Art* (Princeton University Press, 1987), p. 15.

10 It is true that unfortunately in *Aesthetics: An Introduction* and *Art and the Aesthetic* I occasionally did speak of the conferring the status of art as a kind of shorthand for the conferring of the candidacy for appreciation.

11 Arthur Danto, "The 1993 Whitney Biennial," *The Nation*, April 19, 1993, p. 553.

12 Arthur Danto, "Danto Replies," *The Nation*, June 7, 1993, p. 758.

13 Dickie, *Aesthetics: An Introduction*, p. 103.

14 Dickie, "Defining Art," p. 255.

15 For another discussion of Wollheim's misinterpretation see my "An Artistic Misunderstanding," *The Journal of Aesthetics and Art Criticism*, 1993, pp. 69–71.

16 *The Cambridge Dictionary of Philosophy*, ed. Robert Audi (Cambridge University Press, 1994), pp. 378–9.

17 Monroe Beardsley, "Is Art Essentially Institutional? in *Culture and Art*, ed. Lars Aagaard-Mogensen (Atlantic Highlands, NJ, 1976), pp. 51–2.

18 Dickie, *The Art Circle*. This book is the single best account of the institutional theory of art.

19 Ibid., pp. 80–2.

20 Ibid., pp. 9–10.

21 See Paul Ziff, "The Task of Defining a Work of Art," *Philosophical Review*, 1953, pp. 58–78; Morris Weitz, "The Role of Theory in Aesthetics," *Journal of Aesthetics and Art Criticism*, (1956): 27–35; and William Kennick, "Does Traditional Aesthetics Rest on a Mistake," *Mind*, 1958, pp. 317–34.

22 My ideas on this point have their origin in an article by Maurice Mandelbaum, "Family Resemblances and Generalization Concerning the Arts," *American Philosophical Quarterly*, 1965, pp. 219–28.

23 Richard Wollheim, *Art and Its Objects* (Cambridge University Press, second edition, 1980), pp. 157–66.

24 Dickie, *Art and the Aesthetic*, pp. 19–52.

25 Dickie, *The Art Circle*.

26 Wollheim, *Art and Its Objects*, p. 159.

27 Ibid., p. 160.

28 Ibid., p. 164.

29 Wollheim, *Art and Its Objects*, pp. 160–1.

30 Ibid., pp. 161–2.

31 Ibid., p. 164.
32 Ibid., p. 162.
33 Ibid.
34 Ibid.
35 Ibid., p. 165.
36 Ibid., pp. 162–3.
37 Ibid., p. 163.
38 Ibid., pp. 163–4.
39 Ibid., pp. 165–6.
40 Dickie, *The Art Circle*, p. 63.
41 Terry Diffey, "The Republic of Art," *The British Journal of Aesthetics* 9, 1969, pp. 145–56.

5

The Theory of the
Evaluation of Art

In this chapter I move on to the topic of how the evaluation of art is possible. I shall do this by first giving a brief summary of my book, *Evaluating Art*, published in 1988, and then responding to three reviews of that book. My response to the reviews will further illustrate details of evaluation theory as well as demonstrate how philosophical views and arguments can be misunderstood.

In this summary, I wish to impart a sense of my book, *Evaluating Art*. My book concentrates on the theories or theoretical remarks of eight philosophers: Paul Ziff, Monroe Beardsley, Frank Sibley, Nelson Goodman, Nicholas Wolterstorff, David Hume, Bruce Vermazen, and J. O. Urmson. I say in the Preface concerning the work of these philosophers, I try "to organize their insights, to get rid of what is wrong in their theories, to fill in gaps, and to work out a theory that is as adequate as I can make it at this time."

In chapter 1, I outline various types of evaluational theories. I note that the eight philosophers I shall be discussing all hold instrumentalist theories, i.e., theories which attribute art's value to its ability to produce valuable experience. I am concerned in the book with instrumentalist theories. Every theory has certain standard problems it must deal with. (1) Not only must it show how art has value, it must show how individual works have specific values such as being good, being excellent, being mediocre, and the like. (2) Every theory must grapple with relativism. (3) Every theory must have some account of evaluational principles, even if it is only to claim that there are no such principles.

In chapter 2, I outline the historical background of some of the theories I shall be dealing with, but I will not say anything more here about this chapter. I shall also omit discussion of the chapter on Ziff's "Reasons in Art Criticism" and proceed directly to an account of chapter 4 which discusses Beardsley's theory. Beardsley's theory raises all the relevant questions and serves as my guide thoughout the book.

Beardsley's evaluational theory rest on his conception of aesthetic experience. For him, works of art are instrumentally valuable because they can produce aesthetic experience which is valuable. According to Beardsley, aesthetic experience has an objective pole, a work of art with the objective properties of unity, intensity and complexity, and a subjective pole, a person's response which consists of the subjective properties of unity (of, for example, feelings), intensity, and complexity. The objective properties of the work of art are alleged to cause the subjective properties to occur in a person. Thus, a work of art is valuable because it is the cause of a valuable aesthetic experience of which the work of art is the objective part.

Beardsley claims that the objects of aesthetic experience are freed from concerns of the past and future or are set at an emotional distance. This is Beardsley's version of the Schopenhauerian view that aesthetic experience is detached. If a work of art as an object of aesthetic experience has aspects which refer to things in the world outside that experience, then because of the detached nature of aesthetic experience, the referential relations of the work are experientially severed. Consequently, characteristics that refer to things outside aesthetic experience can play no role in the evaluation of art because they do not contribute to aesthetic experience. On Beardsley's view, only the internal, nonreferential properties of art, i.e., the aesthetic properties of unity, intensity, and complexity, contribute to aesthetic experience and, hence, to the artistic value of works of art. Thus, the referential characteristics of works of art such as moral and cognitive content are explicitly ruled out by Beardsley as important for the evaluation of art.

Beardsley believes that three principles are involved in reasoning about artistic value:

A unified work always has some value.
An intense work always has some value.
A complex work always has some value.

Beardsley is aware that the conclusion 'This work of art is good' cannot be deduced using any or all of these three principles. The principles are not strong enough; the principles use the weak predicate 'has some value' and the conclusion uses the strong predicate 'is good.' As a result of the nondeducibility of strong conclusions from weak principles, Beardsley concludes that evaluative reasoning cannot be deductive. He suggests that it is inductive, but he never tries to show that it is. His theory, however, does support deductive evaluative reasoning if one weakens the evaluative predicate of the conclusion from 'is good' to 'has some value.' One then has the deductive evaluative reasoning:

> A unified work always has some value.
> This work is unified.
> Therefore, this work has some value.

But even so, Beardsley's theory, as he states it, cannot deductively support a conclusion such as 'This work is good.'

A careful look at Beardsley's theory, however, reveals that it does involve principles with strong predicates, although he did not notice that it does. Such principles refer to aesthetic experience rather than to properties of works of art. An example of such a principle is

> Aesthetic experiences of a fairly great magnitude are always good.

Such a principle plus a premise about a work of art's producing an aesthetic experience of a fairly great magnitude entails the conclusion 'This work of art is good.' So Beardsley's theory has weak principles with weak predicates such as 'has some value' and strong principles with strong predicates such as 'is good.' Both kinds of principles provide a basis for deductive evaluative reasoning.

I attack Beardsley's theory of evaluative reasoning at its root – aesthetic experience. I argue that there are many cases of proper experiences of art which are not detached, that is, cases in which the referential properties of art have an important role to play. Thus, Beardsley's evaluative system collapses, and both weak and strong principles are left without support.

Chapter 5 is devoted to Frank Sibley's criticism of Beardsley's theory. Sibley's account offers a way to support weak principles. Beardsley has maintained that there are three and only three objective evaluative criteria – unity, intensity, and complexity – and that these criteria always count positively when present in a work of art. I omit detail of Sibley's attack on Beardsley's account of criteria, but Sibley maintains that there are many, many criteria both positive and negative. Sibley also maintains that even a positive criterion may not count positively when present in a work of art because it may interact badly with some other property of the work. Although he does not put it this way, on Sibley's view there are many weak positive principles and many weak negative principles. For example:

> Unity in a work (in isolation from other properties) always has some value.

> Garishness in a work (in isolation from other properties) always has some disvalue.

And so on.

The isolation clause in each principle is there to indicate that, for example, while unity is valuable in itself, if it interacts with other properties of a work in a certain way it may reduce the value of the work. Sibley's view thus allows for deductive evaluative reasoning to weak conclusions.

Nothing Sibley says offers any way to support strong principles.

The main result of chapters 6 and 7, which are on Goodman and Wolterstorff, is to introduce artistic values other than aesthetic ones. These other values are characterized as various kinds of cognitive value or disvalue. (By 'disvalue' I meant not 'lack of value' but the opposite of value.) For example, I characterize what I call 'imitative value.' In terminology lifted from Wolterstorff, I characterize imitative value as value which derives from the satisfaction of noticing that the world of a work of art is true to actuality in some respect. I also characterize what I call 'referent-centered cognitive value or disvalue' as value or disvalue which derives from the value or disvalue of the object, event, or state of affairs that aspects of a work of art represent. An example of this kind of cognitive disvalue is the case cited at the end of Hume's "Of the Standard of Taste" in which a case of religious bigotry is approvingly presented in a play.

Thus, weak principles involving cognitive matters are introduced. For example:

> Truth of actuality in some respect in a work of art (in isolation from the other properties of the work) always has some value.

> The representation in works of art of anything valuable (in isolation from the other properties of the work) always has some value.

Please note that these weak principles guarantee only a minimum amount of value, although in given works of art this kind of value may be considerable.

The principal task of Chapter 8 is to examine Hume's treatment of relativism as it relates to theories that rely on intrinsic valuing as their basis, as mine and the great bulk of the theories I discuss do. The focal point here is that different persons may intrinsically value works and properties of works differently. As noted, most of the theories discussed in the book are based on intrinsic valuing and, hence, threatened by relativism. None of these intrinsic-valuing-based theories, excepts Hume's, broaches the topic of relativism. Beardsley's theory is a clear exception to the intrinsic valuing approach. Beardsley claims that aesthetic experience, which underlies the instrumental value of art, is itself in turn also instrumentally valuable. Beardsley attempts to avoid relativism by claiming that all value is instrumental value and, hence, not subject to differing estimates.

As is well known, Hume develops a qualified judge approach, the point of which is to show that when persons differ, it may be possible to show that one of the differing parties is right. I argue that he is essentially successful so far as differences which relate to the cognitive reliability of qualified judges is concerned. But Hume admits that there are *blameless* differences which derive from our *affective* side; that is, Hume concludes that a certain degree of relativism is unavoidable, and I agree.

The main task of the final chapter is to develop an account of strong evaluations of specific works of art, for example, 'This work of art is good,' 'This work of art is poor,' and so on. Given the acceptance of relativism, these strong evaluations are limited to domains of persons who agree as to the value and disvalue of the properties involved.

Since only weak principles are involved, it is not possible to construct a deductive account in which principles with predicates such as 'good,' 'bad,' and 'excellent' play a role. So some other way must be found to make sense of critics strong evaluations.

My attempt to account for strong evaluations makes use of Bruce Vermazen's account of how value comparisons can be made between *some but not all* pairs of works of art. If a pair of works have exactly the same valuable properties and the rank values of the valuable properties are of a certain sort, then a value comparison can be made of the pair of works. For example, if a pair of works each have the valuable properties A, B, and C and the first work's values for all three properties are greater than those of the second work, then the first work is better than the second. Using ranking numbers for the values this can be illustrated in this way.

First work   (A3, B2, C2)
Second work   (A2, B1, C1)

On the other hand, some pairs of works with the same properties cannot be compared. For example:

Third work   (A3, B2, C1)
Fourth work   (A1, B2, C3)

Each of the three properties of the third and fourth works can be compared to its counterpart, but the two works as a whole cannot be compared. By the way, one chooses a 1, 2, 3 range of rankings or a larger range of rankings for a given property based on the number of ranking distinctions that one can be made in the case of that property on the basis of one's experience of that property. Thus, such ranges are subject to change. One might have to choose a 1, 2, 3 range of rankings for property A and a 1, 2, 3, 4, 5 range of rankings for property B. This means that one has been able to distinguish three distinct ranks of difference for property A and five distinct ranks of difference for property B.

But, even if not every pair of works can be compared, every work can be compared to *some* other actual or imagined work. Assume the fourth work (A1, B2, C3) to be an actual work. Although it cannot be compared to the third work, it can be compared to an actual or imagined work (A2, B2, C3) which is better. Given that this can be done with Vermazen's scheme, I constructed what I called comparison matrices. Using the fourth work as the base work and omitting the letters for convenience, we get, for example, this matrix:

$$
\begin{array}{c}
(3, 3, 3) \\
(3, 2, 3) - (2, 3, 3) \\
(2, 2, 3) - (1, 3, 3) \\
\star(1, 2, 3)\star \\
(1, 2, 2) - (1, 1, 3) \\
(1, 2, 1) - (1, 1, 2) \\
(1, 1, 1)
\end{array}
$$

The base work (1, 2, 3), indicated with asterisks, is better than any work below it and worse than any work above it. The same goes for any work in the matrix. Works paired by dashes cannot be compared.

Thus, for any actual work, a matrix consisting of actual or imagined works can be constructed. I then went on to claim that when someone accurately says that a work is excellent that person is saying that it sits atop its matrix. When a work is good, it is high in its matrix. When a work is poor, it is low in its matrix.

When ranking numbers used get much over 3, the matrices begin to get unwieldy. Consequently, I gave what I called simplified matrices for cases with larger numbers for ranking values. For example:

A B C

4, 3

★(5, 3, 2)★

4, 2, 1

3, 1

2

1

What this amounts to is the placing of each of the base work's independently valuable properties within its own range of rankings. This simplified matrix was supposed to give a sense of where the base work falls in its comparison matrix.

Finally, I want to note two points about my discussion of comparison matrices in my book that have not come up in the illustrations of my summary. In some of the comparison matrices I used zero to indicate that a work lacked a particular independently valuable property. This was a mistake because this use of zero is not a ranking which is the only use that the numbers in the matrices can have.[1] In some matrices I used numbers such as '−1' and '−2' to indicate that a work of art had a particular independently disvalued property. The use of '−' was not intended to suggest that the numbers were anything other than ranking numbers.

I now turn to replying to three reviews of my book, *Evaluating Art*.[2] These reviews are by Richard Gaskin in *The British Journal of Aesthetics*,[3] Francis Sparshott in *Philosophy and Phenomenological Research*,[4] and Cynthia Freeland in *The Philosophical Review*,[5] Freeland's review characterizes my book with such language as "inadept," "major misrepresentations," "absurd," "pedantic," "obsessed," "naive," "potentially repressive." Sparshott's review lacks disparaging language. Gaskin has a few good things to say, but for the most part he finds the book "simply incoherent" and "complete nonsense." Almost everything that Freeland, Sparshott, and Gaskin say is either false or confused. Ordinarily I would not respond to a review, but these three include such serious misreading and distortion that I feel it necessary.

Freeland and Sparshott take me to task for offering a historical account of evaluation that fails to discuss certain philosophers. Freeland cites Hegel, Schelling, Schiller, Nietzsche, Collingwood, Croce, Tolstoy, Marxists, and Freudians.[6] Sparshott also cites Hegel and Croce and adds Heidegger, Ingarden, Lukács, Gadamer, and Adorno.[7] Sparshott writes, "This would not matter if Dickie had explicitly confined himself (as of course he had every right to) to one sort of philosophy. . . . But he speaks of philosophy in general, and nowhere suggests that any alternative ways of doing philosophy of art exist."[8] I was confining myself to the analytic tradition and assumed that readers would recognize this – as Gaskin did. There is no discussion of Collingwood and Tolstoy because I did not think that their views contribute anything to a modern theory of art evaluation. I note that Freeland and Sharshott cite as missing only European philosophers.

Freeland begins with a statement of what she takes to be my overall goal. She says, "in his new book *Evaluating Art* George Dickie stays far away from . . . exciting and timely issues, seeking instead to offer a 'precise' account of how 'to arrive at reasonable specific evaluations of works of art.'"[9] Specific evaluations are only one of many things I discuss in my book. The sentence quoted from Freeland's review about my overall goal is one that she spliced together from two different sentences from two different pages in my book. Most of her pieced-together quote comes from a sentence near the end of my book that reads, "I claimed earlier that there is no better or even any other way at all *to arrive at reasonable specific evaluations of works of art.*"[10] Here, I was talking about the justification of specific evaluational predicates such as 'is good' and 'is excellent.' I was not stating an overall conclusion. The word "precise" in her pieced-together sentence apparently comes from another page where I wrote, "My remarks [about specific evaluations] are a philosopher's account of the logic that underlies critics' [specific] evaluations and what such evaluations would be like if they were made as precise as they could be made."[11] To speak of making specific evaluations "*as precise* as they could be made" is very different from saying they are precise. I was very precise about specific evaluations not being precise but only as precise as they could be made.

Freeland writes, "One goal of Dickie's approach here is to allow the contents and cognitive features of artworks a role in contributing to their artistic excellence. This move is needed, he thinks, to counter a formalist turn aesthetics took when philosophy of art happened to follow Schopenhauer rather than the sensible approach of British theorists of taste. (Dickie never considers the possibility that formalism in aesthetics might be a response to changes in art itself.)"[12] When I spoke of aesthetics following Schopenhauer, I was concerned with his rejection of artistic referentiality, not with formalism. Schopenhauer is not a formalist; for example, nothing in his view prevents the sheer beauty of color from being an object of what he calls aesthetic consciousness. Formalism is a kind of rejection of artistic referentiality but this is beside the point.

Freeman says of me, "He's obsessed with counting: we're told that there are eleven locations for aesthetic experience in Beardsley, and that Hume has thirty-three descriptions of pleasing or displeasing properties."[13] What I wrote about Beardsley is "There are eleven locations in aesthetic experience as conceived by Beardsley at which it is possible to have experiential access."[14] I was not talking about locations *for* aesthetic experience but about locations *within* aesthetic experience as conceived by Beardsley and about how measurement was supposed to work on his account. Also, she fails to note that in citing the large number of beauties and blemishes Hume mentions, I was showing how different Hume's view is from the view of Hutcheson that the object of beauty is the *single* complex property of uniformity in variety. This fact about Hume's theory is important because his advance was in a sense lost when Kant reverted to a single-property theory.

Freeland speaks of my comparison matrices as "byzantine-looking." She also says, "A work having some valuable properties can always be evaluated in a comparison matrix locating it relative to actual or possible works that are slightly better or worse with regard to these same properties."[15] This is very misleading. In a comparison matrix, a work is located relative not only to actual or possible works that are slightly better or worse but is also located relative to works that may be moderately better or worse and greatly better and worse. The whole point of a comparison matrix is to have the complete range of possible works with the same independently valued properties of a certain sort represented.

Freeland writes, "Such comparisons are to be accomplished through an admittedly arbitrary method of assigning numerical scales to valued properties of artworks."[16] There is nothing arbitrary about the assigning of numerical rankings to valued properties; they depend upon the number of distinct differences that an assigner can notice among instances of the valued property. I wrote concerning an illustration of the nature of comparison matrices, "In the discussion above, I have arbitrarily used the values 1, 2, 3. Perhaps a scale of 1, 2, 3, 4, 5 would be better as it allows for finer discriminations."[17] I was pointing out that I had *arbitrarily* used the smaller scale rather than a larger one to illustrate the nature of matrices. Freeland has confused the *assigning* of numerical rankings to valued properties with what I said about the selection of a scale in an illustration.

Freeland concludes, "If interpretation is, as Danto argues, prior to identification of a work of art, and hence prior to identification of its aesthetic properties, then criticism cannot move as neatly as Dickie thinks from a work's *apparent* aesthetic properties to a critical evaluation."[18] This hasty conclusion has no basis in my book; I say nothing about interpretation and do not even suggest that it is irrelevant for evaluation. Interpretation of course precedes evaluation, but my book is concerned with the logic of the evaluation of art, not interpretation.

In a difficult passage that apparently derives from her understanding of what I said about relativism, Freeland asks, "Do critics reevaluating western art from the standpoints of race, class, or gender 'blamelessly disagree' with the more traditional art historians trained in connoisseurship?"[19] I argued that the moral features of art are important for evaluation, so I do not think that a disagreement about an important moral issue such as race, class, or gender would be blameless, as a disagreement over of an aesthetic property such as conciseness might be. Moreover, a theory of the logic of art evaluation should not be asked to resolve difficult moral issues.

Freeland criticizes my account of Goodman's theory as involving "major misrepresentations." She writes that I characterize Goodman "as being engaged in the same sort of enterprise as Beardsley, offering a theory that 'proposes to evaluate art on the basis of its ability to produce aesthetic experience. . . .'"[20] She concludes, "it is misleading to speak as if he [Goodman] places weight on the notion of 'aesthetic experience.' Nor does it help much that Dickie acknowledges that Goodman's view . . . is different from Beardsley's."[21] I said Goodman and Beardsley are engaged in the same sort of enterprise only in that they both present instrumentalist theories. I spoke of 'aesthetic experience' in connection with Goodman because he uses the expression on pages 256 and 257 of *Languages of Art* in discussing symbolization. Not only did I say that Goodman's view of aesthetic experience is different from Beardsley's, I said that they are diametrically opposed. As I pointed out, from the point of view of its historical meaning, Goodman's use of 'aesthetic experience' is misleading and confusing, but he did use the expression, and I was just following him in using it in connection with him.

Freeland writes that I misrepresent Goodman because he "could not be more emphatic about his disinterest in the project of evaluation."[22] She quotes his remark that "excessive concentration on the question of excellence has been responsible . . . for constriction and distortion of aesthetic inquiry."[23] She also quotes his, "a criterion of aesthetic merit is no more the major aim of aesthetics than a criterion of virtue is the major aim of psychology."[24] Even if Goodman had little interest in evaluational theory, his theory clearly has implications for such theory. As Beardsley says of the last Goodman sentence quoted by Freeland, "Even if we concede . . . [Goodman's remark] . . . the fact remains that it [the criterion of merit] is at least *a* major aim of aesthetics. . . ."[25] With regard to the first Goodman quote, I do not recommend *excessive* concentration on evaluation either.

Both Freeland and Sharshott accuse me of misinterpretation for speaking of Goodman's criterion of artistic merit as being how well art signifies what it signifies and of cognitive efficacy. Commenting on a passage I quote from Goodman, Sparshott writes, "The passage Dickie quotes sounds much more like a version of the widely-held kind of theory according to which the cognitive value of art lies in the deployment and development of the means of cognition themselves. But there is no place for such theories in Dickie's scheme, so 'cognitive efficacy' it has to be."[26] I took the expression "cognitive efficacy" from page 258 of *Languages of Art*, and what Goodman has to say about art signifying from the text surrounding that page. Talk of cognitive efficacy is not something that I imported into my discussion of Goodman. Goodman does speak of experiences of art enabling us to see the world in a new light, but art's ability to help us see the world in a new light *derives* from its referring to the world — from what Goodman calls its cognitive efficacy. By the way, I was focusing on the explicit disagreement between Goodman and Beardsley over the significance of art's references to the world for the evaluation of art. I was using Goodman's theory to try to show that Beardsley is wrong on this point.

Sparshott begins, "He [Dickie] makes it clear that an appropriate theory of evaluation must avoid relativism."[27] I say no such thing about relativism. When at the end of my book I give my own view, it is a relativistic one. He repeats his claim about my "anti-relativism" at the end of his review where he writes, "The satisfactoriness of a theory is assessed by whether the author avoids relativism. . . ."[28] These two remarks are made even more puzzling by the fact that in the middle of his review he writes, "Dickie recognizes it as a strength in Hume's theory of taste that he [Hume] admits relativism. . . ."[29] Sharshott has apparently confused the fact that I discuss how some of the theories I was concerned with try to avoid relativism with the view that I think an adequate theory must avoid relativism. But his remark about Hume deepens the mystery.

At the beginning, Sparshott complains that "the question of what art is evaluated for is never addressed."[30] He returns to this complaint right after his remark about Hume, saying that Hume's relativism "might be carried further . . . one and the same person may find different books and pictures equally but differently rewarding on different occasions, in different respects, for different purposes. It is not true that any book can be substituted for any other book that is just as good. It is this familiar fact that makes it so hard to see what purpose [Dickie's] global rankings of works of art could serve, except when prizes are to be awarded"[31] I cannot see why Sparshott thinks my view requires that "any book can be substituted for any other book that is just as good"; it is certainly not a claim that I made. My view about the application of specific evaluational terms such as 'good,' following Vermazen, envisions that many good works of art will have sets of independently valued properties that are vastly different; works of art with different independently valued properties are absolutely not interchangeable. Also, there is nothing in my book that gives the impression that even works of art with the same independently valued properties are interchangeable. In addition, it is possible that the things in Hume's theory that Sparshott wants "carried further" can be allowed for within Hume's relativism. At the end of my discussion of Hume and relativism, on pages 152–5, I introduce a view that is more relativistic than Hume's, and this might allow what Sparshott desires. Finally, my so-called 'global' rankings and evaluations are an attempt to give an account of the logic of what is involved in the application of evaluational terms to works of art. I suppose that evaluations might be used in a variety of ways.

Also in connection with Hume, Sparshott writes, "Dickie misses the point that the qualifications of a good judge of art, as Hume enumerates them, are simply those of a good judge in any field. Hume avoids relativism in this area because there can be little doubt about what qualities people look for in a judge when they actually need one."[32] This is not a point I missed. I give a detailed analysis of the problems involved in looking for a qualified judge. In this analysis, I distinguish cognitive reliability and affective reliability and point out that these two aspects of a judge have very different outcomes for Hume. For Hume the cognitive reliability of a judge is usually fairly easily established, and this is what Sparshott has in mind, but affective reliability is a different matter and is the source of the relativism in Hume's theory of taste.

Sparshott writes, "The tradition whose history Dickie traces is one that takes its start from the confrontation between an individual critic or connoisseur and a work of art as an object complete in itself, and considers the nature and consequences of the resulting experience."[33] Presumably, his point is the same as Freeland's – that I regard interpretation as irrelevant for evaluation. If so, I deny Sharshott's claim. Every work of art that confronts a critic (or anyone else) requires interpretation before it can be experienced and evaluated.

Sparshott makes a serious charge of misrepresentation when he writes, "An author's position may be reduced to a simple statement of one of the alternatives that Dickie admits, no matter how that may differ from what the author said."[34] He gives two alleged examples – Goodman's theory, which has already been discussed, and Kant. His complete statement concerning my alleged misrepresentation of Kant's theory by forcing it into one of my categories is the single sentence, "Kant's account of the aesthetic judgment, for instance, is effectively changed into a theory of aesthetic experience (p. 28), because the concept of judgment has no place in Dickie's scheme."[35] In my historical introduction, I devoted a few pages to the discussion of eighteenth-century theories of taste and how they served as a background for later theories. I said of Kant's theory that "I shall be concerned with the implications of Kant's account of judgements of taste for the experience of art"[36] and then tried to show how certain elements of Kant's view of judgements of taste lead into Schopenhauer's theory of aesthetic attitude and the invention of the notion of aesthetic experience. I was obviously not trying to give a complete account of Kant's theory. For a more complete account, see the chapter on Kant in my *The Century of Taste*.[37]

Gaskin begins in a positive way, saying, "Dickie has interesting things to say about most of these writers [Ziff, Beardsley, etc.] . . . He is at his best when discussing Hume . . . partly because he has sufficiently steady nerves to accept, as Hume did, that no tolerable aesthetic can eschew relativism entirely."[38] Gaskin quickly says, however, that my criterion of aesthetic value "is simply incoherent" because it attempts "to assess the merit of an aesthetic property in isolation from other properties" and that the "phenomenon of interaction between such properties makes havoc" with my criterion. It is not, he says, that aesthetic properties "cannot be assessed; it is that they can only be assessed *in context.*" "It makes no sense," he says, "to ask: setting aside all other properties, what do you think of the tempo of the quartet?"[39] In the passages in question I was trying to do justice to Sibley's distinction between properties of works of art that are of inherently positive aesthetic merit such as 'elegance' and properties that are neutral such as 'contains many puns.' Both kinds of properties may interact well with other properties of a work to produce aesthetic merit or interact badly to produce lesser aesthetic merit or aesthetic demerit. In trying to capture the positive part of Sibley's distinction in the book, I formulated the positive criterion in the following way:

> A property is a *primary positive criterion* of aesthetic value if it is a property of a work of art and if in isolation from other properties it is valuable.[40] ["Primary" was later dropped.]

I then went on to say:

> The isolation qualification is to be understood in the following way: The property being considered is to be considered as if it were the property of a work of art that has only one value property. Please note that the isolation clause of the new definition does not imply that the value properties of works of art are experienced independently of one another.[41]

The isolation clause is an attempt to do justice to Hume's point in "Of the Standard of Taste" where he writes of "the observation of what pleases and displeases, when presented *singly* and in high degree."[42] I talk about the *interaction* of value properties in works in many places and, at the end of the book, I try to work out a way in which such interactions can be taken into account in comparison matrices.

Gaskin goes on, "What are the criteria of aesthetic excellence? Dickie endorses unity, intensity, and complexity, and, following Sibley, adds some others."[43] Here he misses a crucial distinction of the theory developed in my book and that I go to great lengths to emphasize. There are, I argued, no criteria of aesthetic *excellence*; there are only criteria of aesthetic *value.* Evaluational terms such as 'excellence' and 'good' are specific evaluations that indicate that a thing falls on the high end of the value scale, but 'value' is a weak evaluational term that indicates merely that a thing falls somewhere on the value scale. A comment Gaskin makes about unity probably derives from his confusion of aesthetic *value* with aesthetic *excellence*. He writes, "On a sufficiently robust and interesting conception of unity, a chessboard has it and many Braque paintings do not; but Braque was a better artist than the inventor of the chessboard."[44] I made clear that there are many, many properties of artistic merit, both aesthetic and nonaesthetic. That a chessboard is highly unified and Braque paintings are not (if they are not) signifies little according to my account. Braque paintings no doubt have many valuable aesthetic properties that chessboards do not have that account for the fact they are aesthetically better.

Gaskin also comments about unity – "if you stretch the notion of unity to incorporate Braque, the thesis that unity is a merit-conferring property tips over into triviality."[45] In my book, it is clear that I understand unity (as did Beardsley) to be a characteristic that varies from almost zero to one on a scale of 0 to 1. A very low degree of unity will furnish a little aesthetic value and a very high degree of unity will furnish some aesthetic value. A work of art with a high degree of unity can still be an artistically bad work, aesthetically or otherwise.

Gaskin objects that I, citing epistemological reasons, too easily reject objectivism. What I rejected is the view that works of art possess a single intrinsic value property or multiple intrinsic value properties. I took myself to be rejecting a kind of Platonic theory. I did not think at this date I would have to give an argument against objectivism involving an intrinsic value property or intrinsic value properties. Gaskin, however, says that we must accept "a form of objectivism, at least to the extent: given that, phenomenologically, aesthetic experience discerns value in the experienced object. . . ."[46] First, what Gaskins calls "a form of objectivism" is not the same as the "intrinsic-value-property" objectivism I rejected. Second, suppose it is agreed that it is a work of art or an aspect of it is, as Gaskin says, experienced as valuable, the question remains, "Why is the work or an aspect of it experienced as valuable?" My answer was that because we find certain kinds of *experiences* intrinsically valuable and that the *experiences* of some works or some aspects are such experiences.

Gaskin concludes that what I say about comparison matrices and specific evaluations derived from them is "under a spurious shimmer of rigour, complete nonsense." He says he thinks what I say is "mathematically flawed: the phenomenon of total interaction among the aesthetic

properties of a work surely makes the prospects of drawing up and exploit-
ing comparison matrices much more difficult than Dickie allows. But I
won't go into the formalities. . . ."[47] I am aware of the difficulties posed
by interaction and I discuss the problem at some length. Of the "complete nonsense" of my view, Gaskin writes "it is not even in principle possible to make evaluations precise." He explains my mistake: "he [Dickie]
feels the fatal attraction of theory, a tendency which has done great damage
in recent years to the humanities. The plain fact is that aesthetics cannot
be axiomatized. . . . Aesthetics is and will remain essentially a discursive
subject."[48] Gaskin's remark and explanation are not to the point: I was not
trying to make evaluations precise. I was trying to show what evaluations
would be like if they were made *as precise* as they could be made, a sub-
tlety lost on both him and Freeland. I am not attracted to the theory that
Gaskin thinks I am; I am not trying to axiomatize aesthetics. In general,
my discussion of comparison matrices and specific evaluations, following
Vermazen, shows how very limited comparsions of the value of works of
art are and how merely approximate – not precise – specific evaluations
of works of art are.[49]

Notes

1   This mistake was pointed out to me by Bruce Vermazen in his commentary
    at a session of the Pacific Division of the American Philosophical Associa-
    tion in 1988.
2   This response appeared as "Evaluating Art: Reprise," *British Journal of Aesthetics*
    39 (3), (July 1999): 288–96.
3   Richard Gaskin, review of *Evaluating Art*, The *British Journal of Aesthetics* 30
    (October 1990): 367–8.
4   Francis Sparshott, review of *Evaluating Art*, *Philosophy and Phenomenological
    Research*, September 1991, pp. 731–3.
5   Cynthia Freeland, review of *Evaluating Art*, *The Philosophical Review* 101 (April
    1992): 486–8.
6   Ibid., p. 486.
7   Sparshott, Philosophy and Phenomenological Research, p. 732.
8   Ibid., p. 732.
9   Freeland, p. 486.
10 George Dickie, *Evaluating Art* (Temple University Press, 1988), p. 180. Italics
    mine.
11 Ibid., p. 181.

12 Freeland, p. 486.
13 Ibid., p. 487.
14 Dickie, p. 70.
15 Freeland, p. 487.
16 Ibid., p. 487.
17 Dickie, *Evaluating Art*, p. 167.
18 Freeland, p. 488.
19 Ibid., p. 488.
20 Ibid., p. 486.
21 Ibid., p. 487.
22 Ibid., p. 486.
23 Ibid., p. 486.
24 Ibid., p. 486.
25 Monroe Beardsley, "*Languages of Art* and Art Criticism," *Erkenntniss* 12 (1978): 106.
26 Sparshott, p. 733.
27 Ibid., p. 731.
28 Ibid., p. 733.
29 Ibid., p. 732.
30 Ibid., p. 731.
31 Ibid., p. 732.
32 Ibid., p. 732.
33 Ibid., pp. 732–3.
34 Ibid., p. 733.
35 Ibid., p. 733.
36 Dickie, *Evaluating Art*, p. 27.
37 George Dickie, *The Century of Taste* (Oxford University Press, 1996), pp. 85–122.
38 Gaskin, p. 367.
39 Ibid., p. 367.
40 Dickie, *Evaluating Art*, p. 89.
41 Ibid., p. 89.
42 David Hume, "Of the Standard on Taste" in *Essays Moral, Political, and Literary*, Liberty Classics, 1987, ed. E. F. Miller, p. 235. Italics mine.
43 Gaskin, p. 367.
44 Ibid., p. 367.
45 Ibid., p. 367.
46 Ibid., p. 368.
47 Ibid., p. 368.
48 Ibid., p. 368.
49 It has been suggested to me that I might discuss Malcolm Budd's book, *Values of Art: Pictures, Poetry and Music* in this chapter. I shall not do so because our conclusions seem to be pretty much the same. For example, we both con-

clude that artistic value derives from the values that art can produce in human experiences. The books differ primarily in that I develop my view by the discussion of eight philosophers – Ziff, Beardsley, Sibley, Goodman, Wolterstorff, Hume, Vermazen, and Urmson – while, except for Hume, Budd mentions only one or two of these philosophers in passing.

6

Art and Value

The final, or at least my most recent, version of the institutional definition of 'work of art' goes "A work of art in the classificatory sense is an
artifact of a kind created to be presented to an artworld public."[1] Some
seem to think it is so easy to see that this theory of art and its earlier
incarnations are wrong that reasons do not have to be given for declar-
ing so. Here are two recent examples of such declarations. In a review of
a book on aesthetic value, the reviewer, Ben Tilghman, begins with the
comment that the book's author reminds us that "Our ordinary concept
of art . . . is evaluative." Tilghman then goes on to say:

> To call something a work of art is to *suggest* it is worth contemplation.
> Recent institutional and historical theories ignore this value component.
> The author [of the book under review, Tilghman says] is surely right about
> this. Traditional theories, e.g., representation, expression, and formalism,
> defined art in terms of sources of aesthetic value, but did not always explain
> why their defining features are valuable. (Italics mine)[2]

The last sentence in this quotation does not, of course, mean to suggest
that Tilghman thinks that any of the traditional theories is correct, just
that, unlike the institutional theory, at least they are in one way on the
right track. Tilghman begins with the bold assertion that "Our ordinary
concept of art . . . is evaluative," which seems to imply that every work
of art is positively valuable in some way. His next sentence, however,
dramatically weakens the boldness of his initial claim by saying, "To call

something a work of art is to suggest it is worth contemplation." I suspect he thinks that more than suggestion is involved and intends to say that "To call something a work of art" means "it is worth contemplation," which is more in keeping with his original bold assertion. This particular writer also believes, I think, that not much more can be said about works of art by way of definition, that is, he believes that 'art' cannot be defined.

In discussing the institutional theory in an encyclopedia article, Sebastian Gardner makes his intent about the connection between the meaning of 'work of art' and evaluativeness unmistakably clear. He writes:

> it is simply a mistake to separate the classificatory sense of art from the evaluative. Evaluation is just as integral to the concept of art as it is to moral concepts. We do not first classify objects as art, and then discover that they happen to be aesthetically rewarding: conceptually, there is only one move here.[3]

Gardner boldly asserts the evaluative nature of the concept of art and goes on to say that the valuable nature is an aesthetic one. This second writer, however, unlike the first, is friendlier to the notion of a classificatory sense and, hence, to the notion of the definition of 'art.'

Both writers seem to believe what they claim to know with such assurance that they apparently feel that they can assert their claim without any argument or elaboration and then get on to the main task with which they are concerned. This makes it look as if the proponents of institutional and historical theories have overlooked something very basic and obvious.

But what is it that these two writers supposedly know about the concept of art and the class of objects that it picks out? Tilghman claims to know that the concept of art is evaluative and, I think, that the members of the class of works of art are all worthy of contemplation. Since 'contemplation' is typically used in artistic contexts in connection with aesthetic qualities, I assume that Tilghman also wants to claim that the concept of art's evaluative content is aesthetic. Tilghman, I believe, also thinks that it is not possible to define 'art.' Gardner claims that there is a classificatory sense of art but that there is an evaluative element that cannot be separated from it. I take this to mean that he thinks there is a unitary sense of art that is both classificatory and evaluative and which is definable. He also explicitly claims that the evaluative element is aesthetic.

Let us first get clear about evaluation. The scale of evaluation runs from excellent to almost worthless: excellent is at the high end of the scale, with good next to it, with fair below good, with mediocre around the middle of the scale, bad below that, and with the almost valueless near the bottom. I say 'almost valueless' here because I think even the worst art will have at least a tiny bit of value. At the bottom of each evaluation range on the scale is a threshold such that if an object's value exceeds that threshold, it belongs on the evaluation range above – excellent, good, and so on. I have in mind something like the scheme I remember being worked out in Urmson's article, "On Grading."[4]

What level of value do the two writers have in mind when they speak of an evaluative sense of art or the value component of art? One speaks of 'worth contemplation' and the other of 'aesthetically rewarding,' each of which suggests to me a high-end value rather than a lower-end value on the scale I described above. Thus, I take it that when the second writer speaks of the concept of art being evaluative and of art being aesthetically rewarding and the first writer speaks of the value component of art and of art being worth contemplation that they mean that something must exceed the goodness threshold on the evaluation scale to be art – that is, for them, 'evaluative' and 'value component' are ways of specifying 'aesthetically good.' In any event, my taking the Tilghman's 'worth contemplation' and Gardner's 'aesthetically rewarding' as meaning 'aesthetically good' makes their theses specific enough to be discussed. If neither writer regards being aesthetically good as a necessary condition of art, the question of whether it does remains an option raised by their remarks. I realize that there is a range of possible evaluative theories in which the value component that it is maintained to be necessary for art is of a lesser degree of aesthetic value than being aesthetically good, but I am not discussing these theories.

Before continuing, I should perhaps ask what I have done to show that there is a classificatory sense of art to be defined that is evaluatively neutral? Perhaps not much, I have to admit, but there is an explanation and one argument. The explanation is that in 1967 I was led into my view by being a commentator on a paper by Morris Weitz. Weitz distinguished between an evaluative and a descriptive sense of 'art,' and I just took over his distinction and used it. This just shows that commentators use whatever handles are available to them.

The argument I have given is that the theory of art has to allow for a way of talking about mediocre and bad art because people sometimes talk this way about some art. This way of talking pictures the class of works of art as containing excellent art, good art, mediocre art and bad art, and it pictures the concept of *art*, whatever else it might allow, as allowing that art can be excellent, good, mediocre, and bad.

Collingwood had an answer sixty years ago to this kind of move which is that what we call 'bad art' and 'mediocre art' are things that people tried to make into art but failed to. Collingwood went on to say that in talking about art what he was talking about is 'art proper' and not 'art falsely so called.' By 'art falsely so called' he means what he calls 'craft' products and apparently has in mind such things as the plays of Shakespeare and other items he calls 'amusement art' and 'magic art.' (Note that on Collingwood's view amusement art and magic art are not art but are art falsely so called.) By the way, I do not think Collingwood wants to claim that the works of Shakespeare are bad or mediocre craft, and, I should also note, that in some places in his book he does not view Shakespeare so harshly.

I am not trying to saddle my two writers with all of Collingwood's theory, just the part about art as art being good. Also, their claim differs from Collingwood's because they claim to be talking about 'our ordinary concept of art' and not about anything like Collingwood's highly processed and refined philosophical notion of 'art proper.' So, there is an answer to my argument, and it is that what is called 'bad art' and 'mediocre art' are just not art — art as such is good, and this is what I take the two writers to be asserting. It is supposedly not enough to claim that *some* art is good — their claim is that the concept of *art* is evaluative and evaluative to the degree that all art is good, presumably aesthetically so. For example, I suppose that the two writers I have quoted would support the following *kind* of statements, if not these actual statements – 'Cézanne's painting, *The Basket of Apples*, is a work of art, but Frith's painting, *Paddington Station*, is not' and 'Cézanne's later paintings are works of art but his early paintings are not.'

II

As noted, Tilghman thinks that the concept of *art* is evaluative, but does not think that 'art' is definable, that is, that a theory of art is possible. I shall not take up the undefinable challenge here and shall for the most part focus on Gardner's view that the concept of *art* is both evaluative and classificatory, and, consequently, that 'art' is definable.

Assume for the moment with Gardner that the evaluative and the classificatory are inseparable in the concept of *art* and that consequently every work of art is good and that the goodness is aesthetic goodness. What would this mean? One thing it would mean is that the class of works of art is a subset of the class of aesthetically good things that includes other things besides works of art such as the Grand Canyon, a 1950 MG convertible, and other aesthetically pleasing things that are not works of art. One can then distinguish the sub-class of the aesthetically good things that are works of art from those aesthetically good things that are not art within the larger class, that is, devise a way of classifying works of art within the larger class of aesthetically good things. For even if the classificatory and the evaluative are inseparable, they are still distinguishable. But now, how are works of art to be distinguished? Some works of art are representational, so perhaps art is to be distinguished from the other aesthetically pleasing things by being representational. But there are well-known counterexamples to that, so we must move on. Perhaps all the aesthetically good things that are art are expressions of emotion. Again, there are well-known counterexamples. Perhaps the members of the sub-class of works of art are just too diverse to have anything other than overlapping similarities, but then the boundary of the class of works of art becomes so permeable that all sort of things get sucked into the class by their likeness-relation to things that are already artworks. To stop the hemorrhaging of things into the class of works of art, an institutional theory could offer the definition 'A work of art in the classificatory sense is *an aesthetically good* thing that is an artifact of a kind created to be presented to an artworld public.' Alternatively, since some may object to an institutional approach, an evaluative, noninstitutional definition schema of the following kind could be offered 'A work of art in the classificatory sense is *an aesthetically good* thing that is . . . . ,' leaving it up to the objectors to fill in the blank space in some noninstitutional way they desire. We would now have an institutional conception of *art* and a noninstituional schema of a concept of *art* in both of which the evaluative is not separated from, but is distinguishable from, the classificatory. So both kinds of theory could be fitted to an evaluative concept of art by setting the classificatory within the larger evaluative class.

Of course neither of the newly-imagined theories would provide a way of speaking of 'mediocre art' or 'bad art,' but we could speak of things that we might have called 'mediocre art' and 'bad art' as things that persons had tried to make art but had failed to do so because the things had failed to exceed the threshold of being aesthetically good. What could we call these failures? 'Works of failed art' will not do because that would suggest that these things are a kind of art. 'Works of nonart' would not do because it would be too inclusive – including all those things that are less than aesthetically good that no one has even tried to make art. I suppose that we would have to make up a term to pick out just those things that people have tried to make into art but have failed to – perhaps 'works of art-falsely-so-called,' with the words 'art,' 'falsely,' 'so,' and 'called,' connected together by hyphens to make clear that the first word in the phrase does not designate works of art. The above evaluative and institutional definition of 'work of art' can now have a companion evaluative and institutional definition of 'work of art-falsely-so-called.' 'A work of art-falsely-so-called in the classificatory sense is *a less than aesthetically good* thing (*perhaps even of zero aesthetic goodness*) that is an artifact of a kind created to be presented to an artworld public.' Alternatively, we could have a companion evaluative and noninstitutional definition schema 'A work of art-falsely-so-called in the classificatory sense is *a less than aesthetically good* thing (*perhaps even of zero aesthetic goodness*) that is . . . .'

Collingwood and those who agree with him might question why philosophers of art should concern themselves with theorizing about works of art-falsely-so-called other than to note that they are not art. But these works are failures produced in an attempt to produce art, and I would suppose that philosophers of art should be just as interested in artistic failure as moral philosophers are in moral failure. More generally, philosophers would be interested in works of art-falsely-so-called because they are human artifacts of an important human activity. Now that I think of it, Collingwood has quite a bit to say about art falsely so called.

With the newly-imagined definitions of 'work of art' and 'work of art-falsely-so-called,' we now have two new alternative ways of speaking of both art and what we might have called 'mediocre art' and 'bad art.' Both of these new ways present certain problems. Neither of the two new ways of speaking of works of art-falsely-so-called distinguishes *between* what we might have called 'mediocre art and 'bad art,' so, with either scheme we lose some linguistic flexibility. There is also a slightly awkwardness that neither of the new ways of speaking of works of art provides a way of speaking of 'good art' without redundancy. There is a second awkwardness for both of the new ways of speaking, which is that when the expression 'work of art' is actually used as an evaluative term it always or most frequently means 'of the greatest possible value' – the excellent, the magnificent, or the like. Finally, there is another kind of problem in that 'work of art' in its actual use as an evaluative term is not limited simply to aesthetic character, but I will not pursue the question of the value of nonaesthetic elements in art here.

We now have two kinds of institutional definition each of which presupposes the same underlying institutional *practice*, namely, the practice of making artifacts of a kind that are created to be presented to an artworld public. It is worth noting that every theory of art is a description of a practice for producing art. According to my institutional theory, the practice produces works of art. According to the newly-imagined institutional theory, the same institutional practice can have two different outcomes: (1) the creation of things that succeed in being aesthetically good and are, therefore, art; and (2) the creation of things that fail to be aesthetically good and, therefore, fail to be art. The alternative noninstitutional, evaluative definition schema also implies a practice of an unspecified sort with the two different outcomes.

Focusing on the two newly-imagined evaluative theories, it can be noted that the products of the practice of both the institutional and the noninstitutional varieties – namely, works of art and work of art-falsely-so-called – may be very different. Sometimes the product of a practice will be a work of art that is a masterpiece and sometimes the product will be a work of art-falsely-so-called that is awful. On the other hand, sometimes the products will be just noticeably different, for example, a pair of works in which one is a good work of art and another that is just noticeably less aesthetically valuable and fails to be aesthetically good and is, therefore, not art. Whatever the outcome of either practice, each always has the same goal – to produce, to speak redundantly, aesthetically good works of art. But in pursuing this goal, as with any goal, it is known that there will always be failures that fall short, namely, works of art-falsely-so-called. It strikes me that the kind of pair of objects last cited presents a problem for the two newly-imagined ways of speaking in that there could be two works that are almost identical in every respect except that one is aesthetically just noticeably better than the other and the aesthetically just-noticeably-better one is said to be a work of art and the other not. It seems odd to place two objects that are so similar into radically different categories, and this appears to be another mark against the two newly-imagined evaluative theories.

It has been suggested that this last argument, which criticizes the two evaluative theories for sorting two very similar objects into radically different categories, might be mistakenly thought to count against an argument of Danto's that is foundational to both Danto's theory and my institutional theory, namely, the visually-indistinguishable-objects argument, which sorts visually indistinguishable objects into radically different categories.[5] But Danto's argument sorts things in a very different way from the way in which the two theories do. Danto's argument sorts two visually-indistinguishable objects into the radically different categories of art and nonart because the two objects are embedded in two radically different contexts. My argument against the two evaluative theories is that they sort two very similar objects into the radically differemt categories of art and nonart despite the fact that the two object are embedded in the same kind of context.

For purposes of the argument, I began with the assumption that the concept of *art* necessarily involves the aesthetically good. With this assumption in mind, I imagined an alternative history for the philosophy of art, ending with newly-imagined institutional definitions of 'work of art' and 'work of art-falsely-so called' plus an account of the practice that would generate the objects that constitute the two distinct classes of art and art-falsely-so-called. Additionally, I imagined an alternative noninstitutional schema for defining the same two terms, plus an unspecified practice for generating works of art and works of art-falsely-so-called. And, of course, we already had before us my institutional theory of art that envisages a practice that generates the class of objects denoted by the term 'work of art' with no class of art-falsely-so-called.

The two newly-imagined practices would of course also each generate a class of objects that consists of the conjunction of its works of art and its works of art-falsely-so-called. The characterization of this larger joint class of art and art-falsely-so-called, it should be noted, could not have an evaluative component of significance because some of its objects can be aesthetically worthless or almost so. I do not have a term for this joint class of objects. The institutional theory of art used the term 'work of art' for the members of this broad class, but the newly-imagined institutional theory or the noninstitutional theory I am now imagining would have to invent a new term for the members of this larger class, since they have both used 'work of art' for one of the sub-classes of the larger class. Since the expressions 'works of art' and 'work of art-falsely-so-called' have the word 'works' in common and because in both cases an attempt would have been made to create art, perhaps the term 'a-work' can be use for this larger class. Thus, an a-work in the classificatory sense is an artifact of a kind created to be presented to an artworld public. The extensions of my institutional theory's term 'work of art' and the newly-imagined institutional theory term 'a-work' is identical. The newly-imagined noninstitutional theory's definition of 'a-work' also has the same extension as the other two theories. Thus, all three theories in one way or another deal with the same range of objects, although they sort them into sub-sets differently.

III

We now have three ways to talk about art – my institutional way, a newly-imagined institutional way that is evaluative, and a newly-imagined evaluative, noninstitutional way. Presumably Gardner would endorse the newly-imagined institutional theory or the newly-imagined noninstitutional theory sketch. Each of the three ways refers to exactly the same set of objects. Which of the three, if any, is the preferable way of talking? That is, which, if any, embodies our ordinary concept of *art*? The four problems of the new ways of speaking noted above suggest that the old institutional way is preferable, but does the old theory exemplify our ordinary concept of *art*?

First, we need to know what the contents of our ordinary concept of *art* are, since the definition that embodies them would presumably be the preferable one. In the beginning, Plato tried to give our world structure by claiming that our concepts derive from an Intelligible world of Forms, which supposedly enabled us to see the contents of our concepts and their satisfyingly sharp edges. He must have thought of art – that defective and imitative thing – as having no Intelligible Form, just as he thought mud did not. In any event, we seem to have given up on the platonic approach for specifying concepts, but what have we replaced it with? What do the two writers quoted above look to, that enables them to see that historical theories and the institutional theory are confused in trying to define a nonevaluative, classificatory sense of 'art'? Other than claiming that they do not square with 'our ordinary concept of *art*,' they do not say. The only thing that I have previously concluded that could justify preferring my old view as the embodiment of the ordinary concept of art to either of the newly-imagined ones is the argument, already mentioned, that the old way provides a way of speaking of mediocre and bad art and that people do in fact speak this way. And now in the course of this chapter, I have also noted that people speak of good art, as of course they do, and that both of the newly imagined views make speaking in this way sound a bit peculiar because it makes the phrase redundant. In this chapter, I have also contended that in actual evaluative usage 'work of art' always or frequently means 'of the highest value.' All of these remarks are appeals to usage. Finally, I have also noted that the newly-imagined theories place things that are in the same context and that are aesthetically very similar in radically different categories, and that seems odd.

So now the main issue is how usage is a justification for philosophical theories claiming to embody ordinary concepts. First, one needs to ask '*Whose* usage is being appealed to?' Philosophers, who spend most of their time talking at high levels of generality, tend in their usage to go on about such things as knowledge, belief, and perception, about universals and particulars, and also about art and works of art, with the occasional mention of a specific painting or poem. But since it is philosophers who appeal to usage to guide themselves in their highly general conclusions, it is presumably not their own highly specialized discourse that they are appealing to but rather to the less self-conscious discourse of nonphilosophers whose usage would presumably depend on and thereby exhibit ordinary concepts.

Generally, when nonphilosophers speak in connection with art, the actual phrases *used* tend not to contain the word 'art' or 'work of art' but rather more specific terms such as 'painting' and 'poetry' for the simple reason that the nonphilosophers who talk about works of art tend to be either critics who are specialized in a specific domain of art or people who have a particular interest in visual art, music, drama, or some other specific kind of art. A drama critic will, for example, confine his remarks almost entirely to talk that describes, interprets, and evaluates plays. On the occasions when nonphilosophers use the expressions 'art' or 'work of art,' they tend to utter them in a reverential tone of voice that is clearly evaluative and which indicates not the simply good but something of the greatest possible worth. When, for example, a drama critic calls a play a *work of art*, it is clearly to single it out for the highest praise and to mark it off from the more typical fare with which he or she deals. So, the usage of critics and people interested in a specific kind of art *suggests* two different but related conceptions of works of art — a work-a-day conception that picks out paintings, poems, plays, and the like that they are focused on and concerned with as critics, museum-goers, spectators, or readers and another, related conception the use of which is aimed at picking out a small group of works of the very greatest value from among the more numerous everyday works.

I say these usages *suggests* two different conceptions, but the issue is not settled by usage because the different contexts of words, situations, and ways of speaking in which a particular term can be *used* can make a term mean almost anything. So, something in addition to usage is required to explain the stable meaning or meanings that words actually have – the stable meaning or meanings that in part are entombed in dictionaries and that provide the bases that enable us to mean so many different things. We know words have these stable meanings, but how is it that they have them and how do we come to know them? Plato claimed that words have meaning in virtue of ethereal Forms in which their objects participate and which we can come to know by means of dialectical insight. Others claim more plausibly that words have meanings in virtue of more earthly forms – forms of life – and that we come to know these meanings and the core usages that exemplify these meanings by developing within, inhabiting, and participating in these forms of life.

I shall skip over a discussion of the form of life that gives meanings to language in general and take it as a given, leaving the discussion of language in general to more highly paid philosophers. Cultural forms or practices have grown up on top of the foundation of language in general and produce, fine-tune, and stabilize many of the meanings of the terms that are involved within these practices.

Our lives are immersed in practices that direct them into a great variety of channels. There are formal practices of social organization such as government, the military, the legal system, and the like. These practices produce and modify meanings in an overt and explicit manner with edicts, votes, judicial decisions, and the like and these are imposed on the members within the group organized by the practice. There are formal practices of an intellectual sort in which meanings are produced and modified by stipulation, and these meanings are then accepted in a more voluntary way. Despite the occasional manifesto, art as an activity is, by comparison with the just-mentioned practices, an informal one. Or, more accurately, the arts consists of a number of widely diverse informal practices.

Informal practices, like formal practices guide, interact with, change, and stabilize the meanings in the language that accompanies them. Consider the practice of the art of painting. Many object/word pairs, that is, objects and the words that designate them, are imported into the art practice with their meaning relations intact – the pairs pencil and the word 'pencil,' chalk and the word 'chalk,' and brush and the word 'brush' are, I think, examples of such pairs. Other object/word pairs and the concepts that relate them together are shaped a bit by the practice, for example, canvas and the word 'canvas.' In the wider world 'canvas' designates a particular kind of stiff cloth, but within the world of painting it comes to mean that particular kind of cloth cut to shape and size to receive paint. The word 'sitter' in the world of painting contracts in one way and expands in another to come to mean 'a person posing for a portrait.' Thus, as with any practice, language and concepts are created or tailored to fit in with the activity.

No doubt 'art' and 'work of art' – the words of the greatest generality associated with the specific practices under discussion – were derived from or tailored by their home practices. For example, *if* the word 'art' in the wider world at one time applied simply to the production of an artifact, then the development of the practices of painting, sculpture, and the like shaped the content of the concept of *art* by adding conceptual content and narrowing the class of objects to which the word 'art' applies within the discourse of these new activities. *If* 'art' and 'artifact' were at one time synonyms, artistic practices seem by now to have appropriated the word 'art' to such an extend that it seldom appears with its old, broader meaning. So, in this way, art practices could have shaped and narrowed the meaning of 'art' and 'work of art.'

Every theory of art is an attempt to give some further depiction of what is going on in the production of art over and above the actual practices that everyone would agree about. At this point, I shall distinguish between a practice that is envisaged by a theory of art that purports to describe what is universally the case when a work of art is produced, and a practice that everyone would agree is typically, although not necessarily, involved when a particular kind of work of art is produced. An example of the first kind of practice would be that of expression of emotion, which the expression theory of art claims to be a universal feature of making art. Each theory of art would have its own *theory-of-art practice*. An example of the second kind of practice would be that of crafting (painting) a design or representation, which everyone would agree is typically, although not always, involved in making a visual work of art. Each domain of art would have such a typical *underlying practice*.

Do the theory-of-art practices of the traditional theories of art have any bearing on the question of whether *art* is an evaluative concept? If art were made by imitating, then succeeding in producing a representation would produce a work of art and failing to make a representation would not produce a work of art; thus, making art would be a kind of success, which would be a value, and therefore if the imitation theory were true, the evaluative would be part of the concept of *art*. The same would be true if art were made by expressing emotion, which, as Collingwood noted, may succeed or fail.

There are two problems here. First, almost no one today believes the imitation or the expression theories to be correct. Second, and just as important, the value produced by success in representation or expression of emotion could not guarantee a *good* work of art, only a work with a value of some indeterminate degree or other. So, the evaluative element that would be guaranteed by the truth of the imitation theory or the expression theory is not as potent as the aesthetically good that I am attributing to our two writers. In the cases of more recent institutional and historical theories of art, the activities alleged to be at work in the making of art are more a matter of procedure and/or intention and not subject to the kind of success and failure that the practices envisaged by the imitation and expression theories are. Successfully carrying out a procedure of the kind envisioned by the institutional theory or fulfilling an intention does not guarantee that the outcome is good in any degree. If functions such as imitation or expression of emotion were central and determining notions in the making of art, then success in fulfilling the function might guarantee some degree of value, and the concept of *art* would be evaluative in some nonspecific degree. If the procedure of the kind envisioned by the institutional theory or an intention of the kind envisioned by the historical theories were central and determining notions in the making of art, then the evaluative content in the concept of *art* as such would be zero. If the practice that creates art were an institutional one, then the concept of art would not be evaluational.

So, the way in which theories envisage the nature of the practice that produces art has a bearing on whether art itself would be valuable. The practices of the traditional theories might insure value, but such success value would not be sufficient to insure *being good*. There is the further problem that there is no reason to think that success value would be *aesthetic* value. So, the practices of the traditional theories of art, which no one thinks correct anyway, could not insure that a work of art is aesthetically good. And institutional or historical practice would not even suggest any degree of value of any kind. Given the unacceptability of the traditional theories and the nature of the more recent theories, it does not look as if a practice envisaged by a theory of art can inject being evaluatively good into the ordinary concept of *art*.

If, nevertheless, one conceives of the concept of art as evaluative to the point of being aesthetically good, those already-cited problems arise. These problems together with the facts that the most recent theories do not guarantee any value and that traditional theories, although they might guarantee a bit of value, are not plausible, incline me to believe that the concept of art is not evaluative.

Forgetting for the moment theory-of-art practices, let us consider an actual underlying practice that everyone agrees is typically involved in the production of a work of art, for example, the crafting that was involved in the production of Cézanne's *The Basket of Apples*. Does this practice throw any light on whether art has to be aesthetically good? *The Basket of Apples* is by common agreement at least aesthetically good, so Cézanne's use of his practice produced an aethetically good thing. Does that make being aesthetically good a necessary feature of art? The same underlying practice also produced Cézanne's early works and produced Frith's *Paddington Station*, which Clive Bell, for one, thought is not aesthetically good. So, the underlying practice, which everyone agrees about, does not support the view that being aesthetically good is a necessary condition of art. It is of course a possibility that the practice envisaged by the correct theory of art that rides atop the underlying practice will ensure the necessity of art's being aesthetically good. But such a theory is not yet on the scene.

After substantially finishing this chapter, I discovered company in a passing remark in an article by Arthur Danto. He writes of the view that art as such is good:

> Any term can be normativized in this way, as when pointing to a certain handsaw we say 'That's what I call a handsaw,' meaning that the tool ranks high under the relevant norms. But it would seem queer for objects which rank low under those norms to be exiled from the domain of handsaws, and in general normativization must drop out of the concept, leaving a descriptive residue. It is with reference to this residue that works of art were tacitly held to be recognizable among and distinguishable from other things.[6]

It is the residue of which Danto speaks that I have always been seeking in the various forms of the institutional theory I have set forth. And, as has been shown here, even when the evaluative is mixed together with the classificatory in the two newly-imagined definitions I supplied, the descriptive or classificatory residue can still be discerned.

IV

Finally, does there remain anything else to be said in answer to the two writers' contention that the institutional theory ignores the value component of art? Philosophers are almost never completely wrong in their claims, and I am not claiming that the two writers are exceptions. I have taken them to be claiming that our ordinary concept of *art* contains a highly positive evaluative element such that all works of art are necessarily good. For them, the concept of art has what may be called a high evaluative content. The two writers are apparently following an intuition that resembles one of Richard Wollheim's intuitions about art, namely, that 'there is an interesting connection between being a work of art and being a good work of art.'[7] But our two writers' view is inconsistent with another of Wollheim's intuitions in which he envisions that 'a man may reasonably feel some contentment that his life passes in making works of art even though he recognizes that his art is not good.'[8] If Wollheim is right and there could be a lifetime production of works of art, no one of which is good, then the interesting relation between being a work of art and being a good work of art must be a looser relation than I have taken the view of our two writers to be. In addition to being at odds with Wollheim's two intuitions taken together as a set, the two writers stronger view results in several problems of usage. Is there a more painless way to preserve an interesting relation between art and evaluation?

I think a promising way in which being a work of art and being a good work of art could be related is of the following sort – a work of art is not *necessarily* valuable in any particular degree but is the *kind* of thing that is subject to evaluation. This is not a trivial consideration because not everything is subject to evaluation. For example, in the moral domain, a person's killing another person is usually subject to moral evaluation, but the killing of its prey by a nonhuman predator (say, a shark) is not subject to moral evaluation. In some cases, the consequence of such a nonhuman predator's action may be judged to be bad, and we may even destroy the predator, but we do not hold its action to be a morally bad action so that we blame the nonhuman predator.

In pursuing the view that art is a kind of thing that is subject of evaluation, I would want to go beyond the position I am attributing to our two writers and say that aesthetic character is only one of the aspects of art that is subject to evaluation. I can reformulate the institutional definition of 'art' in the following way to accommodate the evaluative element – A work of art in the classificatory sense is an *evaluable* artifact of kind created to be presented to an artworld public. This definition of 'art' incorporates evaluativeness in a way that does not guarantee any degree of value but leaves art open to the full range of evaluative assessment. This reformulation does not, I believe, really add anything new because everyone has always regarded works of art – however they are to be defined – as evaluable; the definition just makes it explicit. I note in passing that the injection of evaluability into the equation harks back to my use of 'candidate for appreciation' in the earlier incarnations of the institutional theory, although the two notions are not identical. By the way, this reformulated definition is more in keeping with Gardner's contention that 'Evaluation is just as integral to the concept of art as it is to moral concepts.' He is right, but he fails to note that moral concepts run the full range from morally bad to morally excellent, so that the actions and outcomes that fall within the moral domain are not all at the plus end of the scale.

The reformulated definition allows us to speak of good, bad, and mediocre art without any problem or awkwardness. 'Work of art' as an evaluative term of very high degree is no problem either. And no pairs of works of very similar aesthetic worth end up being treated very differently. Finally, of course, the strategy of inserting the notion of *evaluability* is also available to the newly-imagined, noninstitutional definitional schema and perhaps to other theories as well.

Notes

1 George Dickie, *The Art Circle* (New York: Haven, 1984), p. 80; republished by Chicago Spectrum Press, 1997.

2 B. Tilghman in a review of A. Goldman's *Aesthetic Value* in *The Journal of Aesthetics and Art Criticism* (Winter, 1999), p. 81 (italics mine).

3 S. Gardner, "Aesthetics" in *The Blackwell Companion to Philosophy*, ed. N. Bunnin and E. Tsui-James (Oxford: Blackwell Publishers, 1996), p. 236.

4 J. O. Urmson, "On Grading," *Mind* 59 (1950): 145–69.

5 A point raised by Peter Lamarque during the discussion period of an earlier version of this chapter, which was read as a paper before the 1999 British Society for Aesthetic meeting.

6   Arthur Danto, "Art and Meaning," in *Theories of Art Today*, ed. Noël Carroll (University of Wisconsin Press, 2000), p. 130.
7   Richard Wollheim, "The Institutional Theory of Art," *Art and Its Objects*, 2nd edn (London: Pelican Books, 1980), p. 163.
8   Ibid., p. 164.

Index